Ethical
Perspectives

Sexual Boundary Issues
and the Chiropractic Paradigm

Ethical Perspectives

Sexual Boundary Issues and the Chiropractic Paradigm

Michael J. Stahl, DC

Instructor,
Loyola Marymount University,
Los Angeles, California
Adjunct faculty,
Southern California University of Health Sciences,
Whittier, California
Private practice of chiropractic,
West Hills, California

Stephen M. Foreman, DC, DABCO

Instructor,
Loyola Marymount University,
Los Angeles, California
Private practice of chiropractic,
West Hills, California
Former Chairman,
California Board of Chiropractic Examiners

LIPPINCOTT WILLIAMS & WILKINS
A **Wolters Kluwer** Company
Philadelphia • Baltimore • New York • London
Buenos Aires • Hong Kong • Sydney • Tokyo

Senior Acquisitions Editor: Peter J. Darcy
Managing Editor: Linda S. Napora
Senior Marketing Manager: Christen D. Murphy
Production Editor: Kevin Johnson
Cover Designer: Armen Kojoyian
Interior Designer: Karen Quigley
Compositor: TechBooks
Printer: R. R. Donnelley & Sons (Crawfordsville)
Design Coordinator: Holly Reid McLaughlin

351 West Camden Street
Baltimore, MD 21201

530 Walnut Street
Philadelphia, PA 19106

The publisher is not responsible (as a matter of product liability, negligence, or otherwise) for any injury
resulting from any material contained herein. This publication contains information relating to general
principles of medical care that should not be construed as specific instructions for individual patients.
Manufacturers' product information and package inserts should be reviewed for current information,
including contraindications, dosages, and precautions.

Printed in the United States of America

Library of Congress Cataloging-in-Publication Data

Stahl, Michael J.
    Ethical perspectives : sexual boundary issues and the chiropractic paradigm / Michael J. Stahl,
Stephen M. Foreman.
        p. ; cm.
    Includes bibliographical references and index.
    ISBN 0-7817-5541-7 (alk. paper)
        1. Chiropractors—Professional ethics.   2. Chiropractors—Sexual behaviour.   I. Foreman, Stephen M.
II. Title.
        [DNLM: 1. Chiropractic—ethics.   2. Sex Offenses.   3. Professional Misconduct.
    4. Professional-Patient Relations—ethics.   WB 905.7 S782e 2005]
    RZ236.5.S86   2005
    174.2′95534—dc22
                                                                                        2004018798

*The publishers have made every effort to trace the copyright holders for borrowed material. If they have
inadvertently overlooked any, they will be pleased to make the necessary arrangements at the first
opportunity.*

To purchase additional copies of this book, call our customer service department at
(800) 638-3030 or fax orders to **(301) 824-7390**. International customers should call
(301) 714-2324.

Visit Lippincott Williams & Wilkins on the Internet: http://www.LWW.com.
Lippincott Williams & Wilkins customer service representatives are available from
8:30 am to 6:00 pm, EST.

05 06 07
1 2 3 4 5 6 7 8 9 10

CONTENTS

Foreword by Richard L. Cole   ix
Preface   xi

Chapter 1   Introduction   1

Chapter 2   Historical Evolution of Professional Boundaries   9

Chapter 3   Positions on Sexual Boundary Issues Among the Health-Care Professions   13

Chapter 4   Incidence of Professional Sexual Misconduct   17

Chapter 5   How Did We Get Here? The Social Pendulum   27

Chapter 6   Absolute Morality and Zero Tolerance   33

Chapter 7   Power Within the Doctor-Patient Relationship   39

Chapter 8   Transference and Countertransference   45

Chapter 9   The Slippery Slope   49

Chapter 10   Sexual Relationships with Current and Former Patients   57

Chapter 11   Legal Implications of Sexual Misconduct   71

Chapter 12   Preventing False Allegations and Boundary Violations   79

Chapter 13   Classifying Sexual Misconduct: A Chiropractic Paradigm   93

Appendix A   Responses to Power Poll Conducted by the Federation of Chiropractic Licensing Boards   103

Appendix B   Role of State and National Chiropractic Boards in Protecting the Public   115

Glossary   119
Index   123

Each state Board of Chiropractic Examiners is charged with the duty of protecting the public by regulating the practice of chiropractic. One of the most serious responsibilities a board has is the proper disciplining of doctors who have violated board regulations and the trust of the public. Sexual boundary violations rank among the most serious breaches of that public trust.

Dr. Stahl and Dr. Foreman first addressed this serious topic in 1997 when the National Chiropractic Mutual Insurance Company (NCMIC) published their first monograph titled *Sexual Misconduct: Ethical, Clinical, and Legal Ramifications and the Chiropractic Profession.* Its publication was hailed in many quarters and was used widely in the profession in areas ranging from ethics classes in chiropractic colleges to advising members of various state boards. Some states made it required reading for their doctors. Other states used it as the basis of new regulatory protections for consumers. With time, however, it became apparent that the chiropractic profession needed to better define where it stood in the spectrum of proper professional boundaries. Without better definition, the profession would be judged according to the standards of other professions.

Their new work, *Ethical Perspectives: Sexual Boundary Issues and the Chiropractic Paradigm,* makes a serious academic exploration of the issue and will help set standards for the chiropractic profession. Difficult subjects such as transference, countertransference, and fiduciary responsibilities are explored and applied to chiropractic. This book will have a serious impact on the profession, guiding those who practice chiropractic and those who are charged with protecting the public. All doctors and students will find benefit in reading and taking this work to heart. Sound advice is difficult to obtain, and many will find clarification of complex situations by following the precepts in this book.

Members of state boards will also benefit from the concepts discussed here. The chiropractic profession requires better standardization in areas such as romantic relationships with former patients. This book will help bring clarity to a difficult subject that is often clouded and charged.

Richard L. Cole, DC, DACNB, DAAPM, FICC
President,
Federation of Chiropractic Licensing Boards
Former President,
Tennessee Board of Chiropractic Examiners

Our involvement with ethics and professional boundary issues has evolved over the past 15 years. It started with our evaluating cases of sexual misconduct and boundary violations and serving as expert witnesses in proceedings before state regulatory boards as well as in criminal proceedings. Each case had opposing experts, with contradictory opinions to bestow upon the judge and/or jury. Typically, one expert claimed "all is well" while the other opined great injustices had occurred. Each side was thoroughly convinced of its position.

We began to wonder how two experts could make such divergent assessments of the same conduct. This led us to wonder how the scientific literature on sexual misconduct and boundary violations could result in such conflicting positions. The answer, it seemed, depended on one's professional vantage point. We found few examples in the literature of allegations of sexual misconduct against the chiropractic profession. The literature we reviewed focused primarily on the behavioral sciences. Their opinions arose from the unique therapeutic relationship between a patient and a psychotherapist. The remainder of the literature came from the medical profession and reflected the unique circumstances of the medical doctor–patient relationship. Similarly, in the past 15 years, we have not encountered objective opinions concerning the power specifically derived from the chiropractor-patient relationship. In the rare instance in which the chiropractic profession had weighed in on the subject of sexual misconduct, there appeared to be a "lemminglike" adoption of standards set by other health-care paradigms.

The extreme differences of opinion and literature, as well as prevailing laws, may have left the chiropractic profession adrift. Are all doctors the same? Should all doctors be held to the same standards of behavior? Do all doctors have the same level of power and influence over a patient?

Is it reasonable to expect that a dentist who sees a patient once or twice a year would have the same level of power and influence over patients as does a psychologist who has had weekly sessions with a patient for five years? In our search for answers to these complex ethical questions, we came to believe that judging all doctors, of all specialties, using the same scales of justice is unreasonable.

Ethical Perspectives is our effort to step back and objectively analyze the literature available on sexual boundary issues within the chiropractic profession. We attempt to determine the uniqueness of the chiropractor-patient relationship and explore the question, is the power of a chiropractor over a patient identical to or different from that of a psychotherapist or medical physician? Each chapter in this book presents a spectrum of knowledge that forms the basis for the final chapter, in which we suggest a unique chiropractic paradigm for classifying sexual misconduct and boundary violations. We suggest that readers go through the chapters in order and suspend their final opinions on the subject until all the information has been presented.

We realize that certain topics create controversy and argument. Most certainly, sexual relationships are near the top of such a list. Nevertheless, it is our hope that the material we present will benefit practicing chiropractors as well as chiropractic students entering the profession and members of state boards charged with protecting the public. The authors believe the information presented here is needed to better serve the profession as a whole. Some who read this work will try to find safe harbor for their own misconduct; that is not the intent of this book. We feel very strongly that the chiropractic profession should decry conduct that is truly unethical and a deviation from our noble standards of practice.

Although this book is an academic work, it does involve a subject that is all too frequently a matter of litigation. Litigation involves lawyers and, unfortunately, lawyers are prone to taking comments and points in a written work out of context. This practice is not appropriate and should be condemned. Any opinions expressed in this book should be taken as a whole and not as an isolated opinion. Further, we have attempted to cover the totality of thought on the subject, and the content of this book does not necessarily reflect our opinion on any specific case.

Introduction

The chiropractic profession may have been taken hostage by forces wielding a plastic ax, a butter knife, and a box of lemon drops. Underlying this seemingly bizarre and nonsensical statement is the justifiable contention that the chiropractic profession has been caught up in the "can't see the forest for the trees" perspective adopted by other health-care professions regarding sexual boundary issues. Moreover, this point of view largely reflects the public's viewpoint of violence and drugs in public schools.

Society has become outraged, and rightly so, at health-care providers who exploit their patients for sexual gratification. Sexual misconduct is reprehensible, and intolerance of it is absolutely warranted. However, in the well-placed motivation to decry these ignominious acts, other areas of the doctor-patient relationship are being erroneously labeled as sexual misconduct. As well meaning as an attitude of "zero tolerance" is, it could place some health-care professionals in danger. This is certainly the case for the unique profession of chiropractic, which is letting other professions and professionals dictate under what standards it is to be judged. We are advocates of many forms of zero tolerance when dealing with true sexual misconduct; but we are fearful that the chiropractic profession may be letting others set its agenda.

■ Current Standards

In setting standards for sexual boundaries and adopting policies for punishing sexual misconduct, the health-care profession seems to have mirrored the widely adopted policy of zero tolerance regarding weapons and drugs on school grounds. In 1994, Congress passed the Gun-Free Schools Act in reaction to several highly publicized school shootings that had occurred across the country. The law calls for automatic expulsion of students who bring a firearm to school.[1] Social factors outside the school yard have also played a role in many public schools adopting stricter safety standards. Clearly, in the wake of the terrorist attacks of September 11, 2001, the nation was put on alert for all forms of violence, and the public's increased sense of vulnerability underlying the strict intolerance of all weapons on school properties is understandable. However, putting "finger guns," a toy plastic fire ax, and a butter knife in the same category as switchblades, guns, and bombs seems ridiculous to rational-thinking people.

Lindsay Brown, an 18-year-old National Merit Scholar from Fort Myers, Florida, was in the process of moving from her family home to an apartment near the college she was going to attend in the fall of 2002. Apparently, during the move, a table knife (with a round tip) fell out of one of the moving boxes onto the floor of her car. A week before graduation, a deputy sheriff spotted the knife in her car, which was parked in the high school parking lot. As a result of the school's zero-tolerance policy against weapons, Brown was taken from her class, handcuffed, and charged with a felony for bringing a weapon onto school property. Her problems did not end there. Brown was also banned from her high school graduation.[2] No mitigating factors were considered. Most notably, no discussion of intent was accepted. The school strictly adhered to its zero-tolerance standards. Taylor Hess, a 16-year-old male honor student from Hurst, Texas, had a similar experience. In March 2002, a butter knife had fallen out of some boxes when the boy helped move items from his grandmother's home to a local Goodwill store. A school security guard found the butter knife in the bed of his pickup truck and notified authorities. School officials recommended a one-year suspension from school because the boy's action "constituted a danger to the other students."[3]

The prohibition against weapons and violence has also extended into the realm of imaginary weapons. Seven fourth-grade boys at Dry Creek Elementary School in Centennial, Colorado, while playing a game of "soldiers and aliens," were pointing "finger guns" at each other. The principal found each boy to have violated the school's zero-tolerance policy against school violence.[4,5] Jordan Locke, a 5-year-old kindergartner from West Deer, Pennsylvania, was disciplined in 1999 because his firefighter Halloween costume included a plastic ax. Janet Ciramella, principal of Curtisville Elementary, stated, "We don't want to encourage children to play with weapons, and we don't want to encourage a tolerance of violence." Jordan's mother added, "I didn't consider the ax a weapon. I thought of it as part of the fireman's costume."[6]

Public schools are also adopting zero-tolerance standards for bringing drugs onto school grounds. In September 1997, a 9-year-old boy from Manassas, Virginia, was suspended 10 days for handing out Certs mints in class.[7] Seamus Morris, a 6-year-old attending Taylor Elementary School in Colorado Springs, Colorado, was suspended for half a day for bringing drugs onto school property. His teacher caught Seamus handing out lemon drops purchased at a health-food store to fellow classmates. The teacher called the fire department and an ambulance, and the parents of the other boys were urged to have their children tested at the hospital.[8]

Should the same zero-tolerance standards apply to both a loaded firearm and a butter knife? To heroin and lemon drops? Although well founded, zero-tolerance standards cannot be applied to all actions in the wide spectrum of human behavior without leaving some victims in its wake. What future awaits the child whose school transcript includes "expulsion for violation of the school's zero-tolerance standards for weapons"? When college admissions personnel review those transcripts, will they immediately reject the student? Will Jordan Locke be denied a college education or a job as a police officer or firefighter because he brought a plastic ax to kindergarten on Halloween? Does the application of zero-tolerance standards necessitate such life-altering categorizations?

Steeped in equally good intent, the current attitudes of zero tolerance appearing in today's health-care literature concerning sexual misconduct mirror the standards associated with weapons and drugs in public schools. Advocates of zero tolerance toward professional misconduct continue to construct stricter policies regarding what could be considered vague human interactions. The evolution of zero-tolerance standards in various health-care professions has been influenced by social factors and contributions to the literature, primarily from the mental health fields.

The social pendulum of sexual attitudes continues to swing in America and throughout the world. A mere 40 years ago, the notion that women should burn their bras was considered controversial, and CBS censors considered Elvis Presley's pelvic undulations so suggestive that the camera crew was forced to film him from the waist up when he appeared on the *Ed Sullivan Show*. These ideas seem almost puritanical today, as billboard ads and television commercials frankly refer to impotence and the benefits of medications promising heightened sexual function. One need look no further than Janet Jackson's half-time show at the 2004 Super Bowl to see the degree to which the social pendulum has moved since the 1960s.

Health-care providers have followed the swing of the social pendulum as well. In the 1950s, the notion of a doctor providing a teenager with contraceptives for premarital sex was socially unacceptable. However, with the advent of the birth control pill, that attitude seems as arcane as the shock over burning bras. Not only is sex education part of the curriculum in almost every high school, but also many public elementary schools have frank discussions about sex and birth control.[9]

The depth of what we have termed the "butter knife syndrome," in terms of professional boundary violations, can be found in the medical literature as well. For example, in 1991, the AMA Council Report stated, "Masters and Johnson advocated that therapists who exploit their power in order to have sexual intercourse with their patient should be charged with rape."[10] Searight and Campbell wrote in 1993, "Recent state laws reflect the perception that sexual involvement with a health-care provider is akin to childhood incest perpetrated by a parent."[11] Each of these statements represents the ideology prevalent a decade before the publication of this book. Searight and Campbell's prognostications appear to have been quite accurate. Not only have laws been enacted that hold health-care providers to very high standards, but also the definition of *sexual misconduct* seems to be expanding to include an increasing number of actions with increasingly serious legal ramifications. For instance, Judge J. Manuel Banales of Corpus Christi, Texas, ordered all convicted sex offenders to place placards reading "Danger: Registered Sex Offender Lives Here" in front of their homes and on their cars.[12] In California, a chiropractor was sentenced to one year in county jail stemming from his conviction for felony sexual battery against a patient.[13] In addition to jail time, he was ordered to pay more than $1,000 in restitution, pay for the victim's counseling, have no contact with the victim, and undergo psychiatric counseling. The doctor was also ordered to register with local authorities as a sex offender. At his sentencing, approximately 20 supporters filled the courtroom. The judge reported receiving more than 105 letters of support from both former and current patients, but he was unmoved by their pleas for leniency, saying, "This is a criminal proceeding; it's not a popularity contest." The judge said he had no doubt that the doctor was a good chiropractor, but he said it was clear to him, as well as an objective jury, that the doctor had acted inappropriately with the victim. "It's clear to the court he crossed the line with the victim and with other patients who testified." The doctor surrendered his license to practice to the California state board.[14]

Just as an ever-widening definition of what constitutes a weapon followed the passage of the 1994 Gun-Free Schools Act, the passage of Megan's Law resulted in an ever widening definition of what constitutes a sex offender. Both of these legislative acts represented the initial movement of the social pendulum of these important subjects. In 1995, a convicted child molester raped and murdered Megan Kanka, a 7-year-old from New Jersey. The convicted sex offender lived across the street from Megan, but the federal law prohibited police from publicly disclosing any information about child molesters. In 1996, Megan's Law was passed and signed into law, allowing public dissemination of information on sex offenders, such as criminal history and residence.[15] The law states, "any local law enforcement agency authorized by the State agency shall release relevant information that is necessary to protect the public concerning a specific person required to register" as a sex offender.

■ Current Literature

A review of the present-day literature concerning the professional conduct of all health-care providers reveals a trend that appears to embrace the zero-tolerance attitudes of many public school systems. While acknowledging the well-intended motives of these attitudes and the standards based on them, we conclude that such standards will lead to intolerance, injustice, and most importantly, a lack of common sense. Although a sexual relationship between a doctor and a patient cannot be tolerated, what if the patient is the doctor's spouse? According to zero-tolerance standards, a doctor in such a situation must bear the brand of sex offender and, in many communities, must register as such with the local police. The facts of such a case are indisputable. The spouse of a doctor admits to being a patient, and the doctor admits to having intercourse with his or her spouse. However, do the doctor's actions constitute a sexual offense equal to that of a rapist or pedophile? Does a lemon drop equate to heroin?

Readers who find it hard to believe that a movement is under way to apply zero-tolerance standards to issues involving professional boundaries might consider the example of a regulatory agency that investigated accusations of inappropriate hugging made against a male doctor of chiropractic. The following is an excerpt from a letter the agency sent to the doctor after its investigation revealed that no misconduct had occurred:

> In these days of elevated sensitivities to issues of personal boundaries, health care practitioners in particular are expected to observe a high level of respect for these considerations. Although the investigator's report has indicated that the episode *was not one of specifically frank sexual overture*, it is abundantly clear that Ms. F's sensibilities were offended, and that the described conduct was not appropriate. As you are aware, this (agency) has a zero tolerance policy related to sexual impropriety and these behaviors have clearly contravened this policy. (Emphasis added.)

The investigation of the events surrounding the allegations resulted in the following conclusion: "A review of the information disclosed in the process of this investigation reveals that there are concerns as to some of the interpersonal practices that you have identified may be the norm for your practice style." It is important to note that this regulatory agency used the generic standard of "health care practitioners." In other words, the chiropractor was not being judged on a standard specific to chiropractic but on a standard applied generally to all medical professions. In addition, merely "offending the patient's sensibilities" was sufficient to violate the agency's zero-tolerance policy. This is an example of how a nonsexual action (as concluded by the regulatory agency), resulted in a formal action. The offended sensibilities, mixed with "heightened sensitivities" resulted in the conclusion that a "sexual impropriety" had occurred, when in fact a simple nonsexual hug took place.

The chiropractic profession is on the doorstep of such zero-tolerance standards, not because of any actions it has taken or standards it has adopted but because it has allowed the attitudes of other health-care professions to stand unchallenged. Chiropractic has stood by with a passive voice in this matter, as it has in other health-care debates. With this book, we hope to begin a dialogue about why chiropractic is unique and why the profession should be judged using its own unique standards.

The research we conducted for this book is more exhaustive than any we encountered in our review of medical, nursing, and behavioral science literature, including some 350 recent peer-reviewed articles covering the complete spectrum of thought on the issues that surround sexual misconduct. In conducting our research, we found that much of the literature presents sexual misconduct and/or professional boundary issues that on the surface appear to have clear-cut outcomes but on deeper inspection reveal ambiguity. This is certainly the case regarding sexual misconduct within the chiropractic profession. The preponderance of the literature on sexual misconduct comes almost exclusively from the behavioral sciences; a small amount comes from the allopathic communities. The legal profession has had to rely on the paradigms of these other health-care delivery systems when faced with cases involving chiropractors. This situation is to chiropractic's detriment but is understandable given that the profession has not set standards for legal consumption.

In Chapter 13, we recommend a new paradigm for change that directly addresses the unique health-care delivery that chiropractic provides to the public. This includes a categorization of unprofessional actions specifically related to the chiropractic profession.

Following the publication of our first work on sexual misconduct and chiropractic care,[16] we were honored to see our ideas being adopted into many areas beyond our expectations. We continued to receive inquires from chiropractic practitioners worldwide and those wanting to establish professional standing in foreign countries, prompting us to publish our second work on the subject. To fully address the issue of sexual misconduct, we expanded our review of the literature to represent a more global perspective. However, because the majority of chiropractors practice in North America, we primarily cite policies and events from that area.

The elevation of the chiropractic profession remains our fervent objective. Although some readers might consider our findings to be an attack on the profession, we have tried to be the champions of truth and clarity. While we take no joy in stating, "The emperor has no clothes!" the fact remains: If not us, who? If not now, when?

Endnotes

1. McLeod M. Zero tolerance means zero slack for students. Miami Herald, June 24, 2001.
2. Ibid.
3. Mendoza M. Expelled student challenges policy. Star-Telegram, March 17, 2002.
4. Barger R. Divine inspiration of the single-issue idiot, part 2. Available at:

http://www.cornerbarpr.com/barrooms/bitingcommentary.cfm?article=1017. Accessed July 27, 2004.

5. Richardson V. Finger-gun families win small victory. Washington Times, May 27, 2002.

6. Lee CJ. School suspends kindergartner whose costume violates weapons policy. Pittsburgh Post-Gazette. November 3, 1998. Available at: http://www.post-gazette.com/regionstate/19981103ax2.asp. Accessed July 27, 2004.

7. McLeod M. Zero tolerance means zero slack for students. Miami Herald, June 24, 2001.

8. DeGette C. 6-year-old busted for candy. Denver Post, November 19, 1997.

9. Sex Education Programs in Michigan Public Schools. Michigan Department of Education. August 1994:11. Available at: http://www.michigan.gov/documents/SexEdPrograms_15101_7.pdf. Accessed July 27, 2004.

10. American Medical Association, Council on Ethical and Judicial Affairs. Sexual misconduct in the practice of medicine. JAMA 1991;266:2741–2745.

11. Searight HR, Campbell DC. Physician-patient sexual contact: ethical and legal issues and clinical guidelines. J of Fam Prac 1993;36:649–653.

12. Thomas CB. A new scarlet letter. Time, June 11, 2001.

13. Marino P. Chiropractor sentenced to one year in county jail. Cupertino Courier, January 14, 1998.

14. California Board of Chiropractic Examiners. Stipulated Decision No. 98-22, April 1998.

15. Violent Crime Control and Law Enforcement Act of 1994, 42 USC 14071 § 170101(d).

16. Stahl MJ, Foreman SM. Sexual Misconduct: Ethical, Clinical and Legal Ramifications and the Chiropractic Professions. Des Moines: NCMIC Insurance, 1997.

Historical Evolution of
Professional Boundaries

2

The prohibition against sexual interactions between doctors and their patients is not a phenomenon of the late twentieth century. Therapies have come and gone over the centuries: trepanning, leeching, and removal of evil humors are ancient treatments long since discontinued and replaced with scientifically proven treatments and instrumentation like radiographs, laser surgery, and magnetic resonance imaging. In contrast, the ethical underpinnings of patient care have remained fairly constant over the centuries.

■ Hippocratic Oath

Admonitions and prohibitions against sexual contact between physicians and patients date back to the Hippocratic oath.[1] *The Oath*, thought to have been written by Hippocrates, is one of about 70 medical texts compiled in a collection titled the *Corpus Hippocratum*.[2] *The Oath* and *The Physician* (another book in the collection) discussed the subject of sexual relations between doctor and patient. The original Greek version of *The Oath*, usually referred to as the Hippocratic oath, stated in part, "I will abstain from all intentional wrong-doing and harm, especially from abusing the bodies of man or woman, bond or free."[3] The oath was rewritten several centuries later for Christian physicians and included the following statement: "With purity and holiness I will practice my art.... Into whatever house I enter I will go into them for the benefit of the sick and will abstain from every voluntary act of Mischief and Corruption and further from the seduction of females or males, freemen and slaves."[4] This oath dictated physician behavior on a professional basis, but ethical lapses continued to occur. In the early days of the health-care profession, sexual relations between physicians and their patients were, in some degree, understandable, because the oath was strictly a promise to attempt ethical behavior, without the force of law behind it. The literature reports no enforcement mechanisms associated with taking the oath.

The fall of the Roman Empire brought an end to the formal medical education that had developed during the previous period. Medical knowledge and practice guidelines were transmitted through apprenticeships in guilds. The guild system resulted in widely disparate practices. The first attempt to reform this "educational anarchy" on the European continent occurred in 1214 with the creation of an annual evaluation of medical competence. Hoping to raise the standards of medical practice, the Earls of Provence in Gaul used this evaluation to take action against practitioners judged incompetent.

The Middle Ages saw the reappearance of a more formalized medical education that attracted a higher class of student from the landed gentry. Curriculum continued to develop, leading to the establishment of a College of Physicians in 1645.[5] Despite continued improvements in education, physicians of the late 1700s endured a bad reputation in the eyes of the public. This was the age of the divine right of kings, and few laws of any type were codified for the protection of the public. The issue of doctor-patient sexual relations grew over fears of the misuse of mesmerism, a hypnotic technique introduced by the German physician Franz Mesmer. The official concern was that physicians would misuse hypnosis to take sexual advantage of their patients. The unofficial concern was that King Louis XVI was not nearly as enthralled with Mesmer as was the queen who was being hypnotized.

■ Freud and His Followers

Eventually, Mesmer was officially discredited, but concern over sexual relations between doctor and patient continued even outside the royal court. Ernest Jones, a colleague and biographer of Freud, described erotic interactions between therapists and their patients in one of the earliest reports of psychotherapy.[6] One case, which occurred in 1880, involved therapist Joseph Breuer's use of hypnosis to treat hysterical reactions in one of his patients, Anna O. It seems that Breuer developed what would now be termed a strong countertransference (which will be discussed in Chapter 8). Sexual feelings between therapists and patients were later acknowledged by Freud.[7] He labeled the romantic feelings of his female patients towards him as transference and noted that "therapists should not take advantage of the patient's 'longing for love' and should abstain from sexual involvement."[8]

The behavioral sciences continued to be the focus of attention and the primary source of reporting in the literature on issues of sexual relations between doctors and patients in the twentieth century. Despite the early warnings of Freud, his followers and others continued to experiment with the possible therapeutic benefits of sex in the psychoanalytic relationship. Sandor Ferenczi, a follower of Freud, engaged in kissing and other physical contact with patients, resulting in a strongly worded letter from Freud in 1931, warning him about his actions.[9] Wilhelm Reich, another follower of Freud, wrote in 1945 that the therapist should allow the client's sexual feelings to develop until they are "concentrated, without ambivalence, in the transference."[10] Reich never advocated overt sexual relationships but did admit that he would "physically manipulate a patient to the appropriate response." This approach was controversial and also received condemnation. American psychiatrist Judd Marmor condemned the practice and accused Reich and his followers of using "the prestige of this unfortunate psychoanalytic pioneer to act out their own counter-transference needs."[11]

The issue of sexual boundaries continued to develop and accelerate in the 1960s and 1970s. William Masters and Virginia Johnson, for example, gathered data from many research participants for their 1966 and 1970 reports *Human Sexual Response* and *Human Sexual Inadequacy*, respectively.[12,13] They were surprised at the number of participants in their samples who had engaged in sex with therapists. At this time, patients were starting to strike back against therapists in court. The 1976 case of *Roy v. Hartogs* was one of the first cases in which a patient successfully brought suit against her therapist for sexual relations.[14] In the case, the patient sought therapy because of sexual problems. At her therapist's suggestion, sex became part of the treatment that lasted 13 months. The patient claims this worsened her condition to the extent that she was twice confined to a mental institution. The court concluded that the "relationship between psychiatrist and patient is analogous to the guardian-ward relationship . . . that a guardian cannot claim that a ward is capable of consenting." The court also stated, "Thus, from

[Freud] to the modern practitioner we have common agreement of the harmful effects of sensual intimacies between patient and therapist."

Endnotes

1. Campbell ML. The oath: an investigation of the injunction prohibiting physician-patient sexual relations. Perspect Biol Med 1989;32:300–308.
2. Schoener GR. Sexual exploitation: historical overview. In: Proceedings of the 2nd International Conference on Sexual Exploitation by Professionals. Minneapolis: October 1992.
3. Reiser SJ, Dyck AJ, Curra WJ. Ethics in Medicine—Historical Perspectives and Contemporary Concerns. Cambridge, MA: MIT Press, 1977.
4. Braceland F. Historical perspectives of the ethical practice of psychiatry. Am J Psych 1969;125:230–237.
5. Schoener GR. Breach of Trust. Thousand Oaks, CA: Sage, 1994.
6. Jones E. The Life and Work of Sigmund Freud. Vol. 1. New York: Basic Books, 1953.
7. Freud S. Introductory Lectures in Psychoanalysis. 1917. W.W. Norton & Company, NY, NY. This republication was done in 1990. ISBN 0-393-00743-X.
8. Schoener GR. Breach of Trust. Thousand Oaks, CA: Sage, 1994.
9. Grosskurth P. The Secret Ring: Freud's Inner Circle and the Politics of Psychoanalysis. Reading, MA: Addison-Wesley, 1991.
10. Reich W. Character Analysis. New York: Orgone Institute, 1945.
11. Marmor J. The seductive psychotherapist. Psychiatry Digest 1970; 31:10–16.
12. Masters W, Johnson V. Human Sexual Response. Boston: Little Brown, 1966.
13. Masters W, Johnson V. Human Sexual Inadequacy. Boston: Little Brown, 1970.
14. Roy v Hartogs, 85 Misc.2d 891, 381NYS 2d 587, 588 (1976).

Positions on Sexual Boundary Issues Among the Health-Care Professions

Throughout the world, vast numbers of people afflicted with a wide variety of mental and physical ailments seek care from a large assortment of health-care providers. Physicians, nurses, chiropractors, therapists— all interact with the sick in a manner guided by a particular set of rules. In some respects, the interaction rules are the same for all types of health-care providers, but in other respects, there are vast differences. The variations stem from differences in licensing authority, scope of practice, power influence, and even practice location. In this chapter, we review the rules on doctor-patient interactions developed by several health-care professional organizations to better understand the chiropractic paradigm of doctor-patient relations.

■ Physician and Psychotherapist Organizations

The issue of sexual relationships between doctor and patient has developed in many different arenas. In 16 states, sexual relations between psychotherapists and patients now carry criminal penalties.[1] Professional associations have also entered the picture and have commented on the propriety of doctor-patient sexual relations. The American Medical Association (AMA) initially addressed the issue in 1989 when it passed its first ethical rule prohibiting sexual contact between physicians and patients.[2] Taken in reaction to increasing public, judicial, and legislative attention to the issue, this first step gave rise to increased accountability and higher standards of conduct. The AMA expanded its 1989 ethical opinion in 1991 to prohibit physician sexual contact with former patients for an indefinite period "if the physician uses or exploits the trust, knowledge, emotions, or influence derived from the previous professional relationship."[3] This caveat appears to be an attempt to prohibit sexual contact with former patients in cases when the previous doctor-patient relationship placed the doctor in a position of advantage.

Similar ethical rules against sexual contact between professionals and patients have been encountered in the behavioral sciences. In the same year the AMA prohibited physicians from having sexual contact with former patients, the Revisions Task Force of the American Psychological Association instituted a specific prohibition against sexual contact with former clients.[4]

Other countries have also established bans against doctor-patient sexual relations. The 1990 Canadian Medical Association (CMA) Code of Ethics held that physicians should not exploit their patients and to "consider first the well-being of the patient."[5] Canadian provinces then began developing their own positions on the issue. Ontario published its position in 1991 and British Columbia in 1992.[6,7] In 1994, the CMA expanded its policy to specifically state, "Physicians should never be sexually or romantically involved with their current patients.... The propriety of a physician entering into a sexual or romantic relationship with a former patient should be judged on a case-by-case basis."[8] No specific "cooling-off" period was endorsed by the CMA, but the "amount of time that has passed since service ceased" was suggested as one of the factors to be used in consideration of sexual misconduct.

■ Nursing Organizations

As late as 1993, sexual relations between nurses and patients was not directly addressed by the American Nursing Association (ANA) Code of Ethics.[9] According to the ANA, however, its code of ethics contains an implied restriction of nurses engaging in sexual relations with patients.

■ Chiropractic Organizations

Like the other health-care professional associations, the American Chiropractic Association (ACA) has developed policies and codes of ethics to address the propriety of doctor-patient sexual contact. In 1991, the ACA approved the following addition to its code of ethics:

> The physician-patient relationship requires the doctor of chiropractic to exercise utmost care that he or she will do nothing to "exploit the trust and dependency of the patient." Doctors of chiropractic should make every effort to avoid dual relationships that could impair their professional judgment or risk the possibility of exploiting the confidence placed in them by the patient.[10]

The ambiguous nature of this language resulted in numerous requests to clarify the ACA position regarding sexual intimacies between doctor and patient. The ACA Ethics Committee offered an advisory opinion on the subject and stated that "sexual intimacies with a patient are unprofessional and unethical based on the existing ethical provisions in the ACA Code of Ethics: A(6), A(7), A(10) and C(2)."

The International Chiropractic Association (ICA) also has a code of ethics with generalized language that could be interpreted to prohibit doctor-patient sexual relationships: "The doctor of chiropractic shall not take physical, emotional or financial advantage of the public or any patient he/she serves."[11]

Over the years, chiropractic regulatory boards in the United States have also developed prohibitions against chiropractor-patient sexual relations. A power poll conducted by the Federation of Chiropractic Licensing Boards (FCLB) revealed that 35 of 41 states responding had "some" regulations concerning doctor-patient sexual relations, although only 25 states had specific language in their laws that addressed the issue (Federation of Chiropractic Licensing Boards, unpublished data, 2002). Appendix A summarizes the complete results of the power poll.

It is incumbent on the chiropractic profession to recognize that sexual relations between doctor and patient is an issue that spans all areas of health care. Chiropractic is being swept along with changes in policies enacted by various groups, sometimes to the detriment of the profession. The objective of this book is to shed light on the differences and similarities between the chiropractic profession, the medical profession, and the behavioral sciences. The differences should encourage the development of a chiropractic paradigm for assessing the interactions between doctors of chiropractic and their patients.

Endnotes

1. Bloom JD, Nadelson CC, Notman MT, eds. Physician Sexual Misconduct. Washington DC: American Psychiatric Press, 1999.
2. American Medical Association Council on Ethical and Judicial Affairs. Opinion 8.14: Sexual Misconduct. Chicago: American Medical Association, 1989.
3. American Medical Association Council on Ethical and Judicial Affairs. Sexual misconduct in the practice of medicine. JAMA 1991;266:2741–2745.
4. Shopland SN, VandeCreek L. Sex with ex-clients: theoretical rationales for prohibition. Ethics Behav 1991;1(1):35–44.
5. The patient-physician relationship and the sexual abuse of patients. CMAJ 1994;150:1884A–1884F.
6. Final report of the task force on sexual abuse of patients. Toronto, Ontario: College of Physicians and Surgeons of Ontario, 1991.
7. Crossing the boundaries: the report of the committee on physician sexual misconduct. Vancouver, BC: College of Physicians and Surgeons of British Columbia, 1992.
8. Canadian Medical Association Policy Summary. The patient-physician relationship and the sexual abuse of patients. Can Med Assoc J 1994;150(11):1884–1885.
9. Pennington S, Gafner G, Schilit R, Bechtel B. Addressing ethical boundaries among nurses. Nurse Manage 1993;24(6):36–39.
10. American Chiropractic Association Code of Ethics, A(6), A(7), A(10), and C(2), 1991.
11. International Chiropractic Association Code of Ethics, principle 1K., 1993.

Incidence of Professional Sexual Misconduct

Is the problem of sexual misconduct between doctors and patients as bad as it seems? The answer to this commonly asked question is a critical part of analyzing social boundary issues in the chiropractic profession. Some people insist the problem is overstated, and they point to multiple sources repeatedly citing the same few cases. Others would contend the problem is greatly underreported. To better understand the actual incidence of these problems, it is important to review the available sources and their data collection methods.

The available literature on the incidence of sexual misconduct focuses on the mental health fields and the allopathic communities. A review of the literature reveals that in most cases, data was collected through the use of anonymous surveys sent to practitioners through the mail. Two survey methods were used. The first method was to ask practitioners about their own personal involvement with patients. The second method was to ask practitioners how many of their patients had reported some type of boundary violation by another practitioner. Although the second type of survey may have some value, it is inherently flawed because it did not account for the patient who receives care from multiple practitioners and reports the same incidence of alleged sexual misconduct on multiple occasions. A thorough review of cited incidence rates must weigh the quality of the investigations against the reported findings. Because all incidence rates for sexual misconduct reported in the literature involve, at best, informed guesses, the methodologies used to determine the rates are seriously flawed.

A review of the most prominent incidence rates reported in the literature over the past 25 years revealed a fairly consistent rate of reported sexual involvement with patients. Among male clinicians, a rate of

5% to 10% was reported most often; and among female clinicians, the range was from 0.5% to 3%. However, a close review of the reported studies fails to demonstrate agreement on the definitions of *sexual misconduct* and *boundary violations*.[1] To bring clarity to the subject, we reviewed studies conducted in various countries and focusing on various specialties. We present these studies in chronological order to demonstrate differences in the responses and occurrences with the passage of time.

■ United States: Behavioral Sciences

One of the earliest studies to quantify the incidence rate of sexual misconduct between physicians and patients was reported in 1973. This survey of male psychiatrists, obstetricians, gynecologists, surgeons, internists, and general practitioners licensed in California was undertaken by Kardener, Fuller, and Mensh.[2] The researchers found that 5% to 13% (the range accounts for all specialties) of respondents had engaged in noncoital activity with patients, and 5% to 7% had been involved in coital activity.

Holroyd and Brodsky surveyed licensed doctoral-level psychologists, both male and female.[3] Among male respondents, 5.5% indicated they had had coital relationships with patients, while only 0.6% of female respondents reported such activity. The study also found that 2.6% of male respondents and 0.3% of female respondents had had sexual relations with patients within 3 months of terminating treatment. Finally, 80% of the respondents who admitted engaging in sexual activity with patients had done so with more than one patient.

In a 1979 survey, Pope, Levenson, and Schover reported that 7% of the responding psychologists had been sexually involved with patients.[4] Bouhoutsos, Holroyd, Lerman, Forer, and Greenberg surveyed California licensed psychologists in 1983.[5] They reported that 4.8% of men responding to the survey and 0.8% of women had been sexually involved with patients. In addition, 13.7% of men and 3.1% of women reported having engaged in some form of intimacy with their psychotherapy clients. Among psychiatric residents, 4.9% said they had had sexual relations with their supervisors during training.

Gartrell, Herman, Olarte, Feldstein, and Localio conducted a survey of 1,400 psychiatrists in 1986.[6] The researchers found that approximately 7% of male psychiatrists and 3% of female psychiatrists admitted having sexual contact with clients. The gender breakdown of the reported sexual contact was as follows: 88% occurred between male psychiatrists and female patients; 7.6% between male psychiatrists and male patients; 3.5% between female psychiatrists and male patients; and 1.4% between female psychiatrists and female patients. The reported sexual contact occurred in most cases during treatment or within 6 months of termination of treatment.

Akamatsu surveyed 1,400 psychiatrists in 1988 and reported that 65% had treated a patient who admitted to sexual involvement with a previous therapist.[7] Brodsky found a range of 3.6% to 12.1% of male psychologists in the United States reportedly having had some sexual intimacy with clients; among female psychologists, the range was 0.5% to 2.6%.[8]

Parsons and Wineze surveyed licensed mental health professionals in Rhode Island and reported in 1995 that 26% of respondents had treated a patient who had been sexually abused by a former therapist.[9] This study defined *mental health professionals* as psychologists, psychiatrists, social workers, marriage and family therapists, and mental health counselors. However, it did not define the term *sexual involvement*, which they admitted may have resulted in a bias in their conclusions.After comparing their survey results to the number of complaints and eventual disciplinary actions taken by the state regulatory board, the researchers concluded that only 3% of cases of sexual misconduct were reported to state regulatory boards. This type of underreporting, using regulatory board accusations and disciplinary numbers, correlated with other surveys as well.

In summary, the surveys of mental health professionals show a bias regarding the social, political, and cultural attitudes seen in the United States over the past 20 years. Galletly concluded, "Most of the research in this area has been undertaken in the USA."[10] As a result, the cultural perceptions of sexuality may be skewed in the reported medical literature.

■ United States: Medical Professions

Dehlendorf and Wolfe reviewed 761 cases of physicians disciplined for sex-related offenses in the United States from 1981 through 1996.

TABLE 4-1 ■ SELECTED SPECIALTIES OF PHYSICIANS DISCIPLINED FOR SEX-RELATED OFFENSES, 1989–1995

SPECIALTY	PHYSICIANS DISCIPLINED	PHYSICIANS IN SPECIALTY NATIONALLY
Psychiatry	133	36,405
Child psychiatry	12	4,618
Obstetrics and gynecology	60	35,273
Family and general practice	97	71,688
Emergency medicine	12	15,470
Orthopedic surgery	11	20,640
Internal medicine	43	109,107
Anesthesiology	9	28,148
Pediatrics	14	44,881
General surgery	17	39,211
Total	477	578,108

Adapted from Dehlendorf CE, Wolfe S. Physicians disciplined for sex-related offenses. JAMA 1998;279(23):1883–1888.

Forty-two occurrences were reported in 1989 and 147 in 1996. Of the 761 physicians disciplined during the review period, 75% involved sexual intercourse, rape, molestation, or sexual favors for drugs. The specialties of the physicians disciplined for sex-related offenses were psychiatry, child psychiatry, obstetrics and gynecology, and family and general practice (listed in decreasing order of prevalence).[11] Table 4-1 summarizes the results of Dehlendorf and Wolfe's review.

In 1992 Gartrell, Milliken, Goodson, Thiemann, and Lo conducted a survey of family practitioners, internists, obstetricians and gynecologists, and surgeons.[12] Nine percent of the respondents acknowledged sexual contact with one or more patients. Ten percent of male respondents reported sexual contact with patients compared with 4% of female respondents. In terms of specialties, the incidence rates were 11% of family practitioners, 10% of obstetricians and gynecologists, 9% of surgeons, and 6% of internists. Eighty-nine percent of the sexual contact occurred between male doctors and female patients, 6% between female doctors and male patients, 4% between male doctors and male patients, and 1% between female doctors and female patients.

Gartrell and colleagues also found that 63% of respondents to their survey considered sexual contact "always harmful," and 94% opposed sexual contact with current patients while 37% opposed sexual contact with former patients. Fifty-six percent of physicians surveyed indicated that the issue of doctor-patient sexual contact had never been addressed in their training. More than half agreed with and favored rules by state regulating boards to prohibit physician-patient sexual contact.

■ Canada: Behavioral Sciences

A 1991 survey of Canadian psychiatric residents was reported by Carr, Robinson, Stewart, and Kussin.[13] These authors investigated sexual contact between residents and educators during the training period. Of the 314 respondents to confidential questionnaires, 4.1% of female residents and 1.2% of male residents reported sexual involvement with their educators. Most of those reporting this type of involvement said they had positive or neutral feelings about relationships they had had before their involvement with the educators. All reported relationships were heterosexual.

■ Canada: Medical Professions

A survey conducted among Canadian obstetricians and gynecologists found that 10% of respondents were aware of a colleague having been sexually involved with a patient.[14] Three percent of male respondents and 1% of female respondents reported sexual involvement with patients. For a proven sexual impropriety, a reprimand and fine was supported by 33% of those responding, and 57% supported the license revocation for a proven sexual transgression and 74% for a proven sexual violation. (The three escalatory categories of sexual misconduct are discussed in greater detail in Chapter 9.)

■ Canada: Nursing

The College of Nurses of Ontario received 32 complaints for sexual issues between 1993 and 1995. Gallop found that male staff were more likely to become sexually involved with patients and that the involvement included instances of coercing patients and claiming sexual behavior was "therapy."[15] Female nurses who became sexually involved with patients were more likely to harbor "rescue fantasies" about their involvement, believing it could "save" the patient.

■ Israel: Behavioral Sciences and Medical Profession

Rubin and Dror conducted a survey from 1992 to 1993 with 272 physicians and 263 clinical psychologists.[16] Thirty-four percent responded to the survey. The majority of those who responded had studied or were studying in Israel. The physicians included all specialties except psychiatry and obstetrics and gynecology. Three percent of psychologists and 14.5% of physicians reported being involved in a "sexualized practice."

■ Australia and Rhode Island: Behavioral Sciences

In 1996, Wincze, Richards, Parsons, and Bailey published a survey of licensed psychologists in Rhode Island and Western Australia.[17] Despite distinct cultural and training differences, very similar results were obtained as to the treatment of patients who had been victims of sexual abuse.

■ Chiropractic Profession

A review of the literature failed to reveal any published incidence rate of sexual abuse between chiropractors and their patients (either current or former). Foreman and Stahl conducted a retrospective analysis of 216 chiropractors disciplined for various reasons in California between January 1998 and April 2002 and then separated them into relevant categories.[18] Of the 216 cases, 49 (22.6%) were for sexual offenses or boundary violations. By comparison, Morrison and Wickersham reviewed 375 disciplinary actions against medical doctors in California and found that 37 (10%) of the 375 disciplinary actions were for sexual boundary violations.[19] At first glance, it would appear that the rate for chiropractors was slightly more than double that for medical doctors. However, a valid comparison must account for the difference between the number of chiropractors and the number of medical doctors. The incidence rate of disciplinary actions against California medical doctors was 0.23 incidents per 1,000 doctors per year. The incidence rate of disciplinary actions against California chiropractors was 1.01 per 1,000 doctors per year. Using equally weighted figures reveals that the sexual misconduct disciplinary rate for chiropractors in California was 339% higher than their medical counterparts.

Public complaints to a chiropractic board can also be used to assess incidence rates, even though these allegations have not been fully adjudicated. In 2002, Budnick reviewed complaints of sexual misconduct filed with various regulatory boards in Oregon (see Table 4-2).[20] The incidence rate of sexual complaints per 1,000 licensed doctors was highest in the chiropractic profession at 30.5 per 1,000. This was roughly 200% higher than the 10.3 complaints per 1,000 licensees at the Board of

TABLE 4-2 ■ COMPLAINTS OF SEXUAL MISCONDUCT FILED AGAINST LICENSED SOCIAL WORKERS AND HEALTH-CARE PROVIDERS IN OREGON, 1998–2002

LICENSING BOARD	LICENSES	COMPLAINTS	RATE PER 1,000 PROVIDERS
Board of Chiropractic Examiners	1,575	48	30.5
Board of Licensed Professional Counselors and Therapists	1,365	14	10.3
Board of Psychologist Examiners	1,149	7	6.1
Board of Clinical Social Workers	2,862	17	5.9
Board of Massage Therapists	4,111	22	5.4
Board of Medical Examiners	13,658	45	3
Board of Nursing	62,628	110	1.8
Board of Dentistry	6,698	2	0.3

Note: Figures were provided by each licensing board. Board of Nursing data are estimates based on fiscal-year data.
Adapted from Budnik N. Can't touch this. Willamette Weekly Online, November 27, 2002.

Licensed Professional Counselors and Therapists. Stemming the ominous trend of chiropractic providers accused and disciplined for sexual misconduct requires a serious attempt to identify the genesis of the problem.

Endnotes

1. Parsons J, Wineze JP. Survey of client-therapist sexual involvement in Rhode Island as reported by subsequent treating therapists. Prof Psychol Res Pr 1995;26:171–175.
2. Kardener SH, Fuller M, Mensh IN. A survey of physician's attitudes and practices regarding erotic and no-erotic contact with patients. Am J Psychiatry 1973;130:1077–1108.
3. Holroyd JC, Brodsky AM. Psychologists' attitudes and practices regarding erotic and non-erotic physical contact with patients. Am Psychol 1977;32:843–849.
4. Pope KS, Levenson H, Schover LR. Sexual intimacy in psychology training: results and implications of a national survey. Am Psychol 1979;34:682–689.
5. Bouhoutsos JC, Holroyd JC, Lerman H, Forer BR, Greenberg M. Sexual intimacy between psychotherapists and patients. Prof Psychol Res Pr 1983;14:185–196.
6. Gartrell N, Herman JL, Olarte S, Feldstein M, Localio R. Psychiatrist-patient sexual contact. Results of a national survey I: prevalence. Am J Psychiatry 1986;43:1126–1131.
7. Akamatsu JT. Intimate relationships with former clients: national survey of attitudes and behavior among practitioners. Prof Psychol Res Pr 1988;19:454–458.
8. Brodsky AM. Sex between patient and therapist: psychology's data and response. In: Gabbard GO, ed. Sexual Exploitation in Professional Relationships. 1st Ed. Washington, DC: American Psychiatric Press 1989:15–25.
9. Parsons J, Wineze JP. Survey of client-therapist sexual involvement in Rhode Island as reported by subsequent treating therapists. Prof Psychol Res Pr 1995;26:171–175.
10. Galletly CA. Psychiatrist-patient sexual relationships: the ethical dilemmas. Aust N Z J Psychiatry 1993;27:133–139.
11. Dehlendorf CE, Wolfe S. Physicians disciplined for sex-related offenses. JAMA 279:1883–1888.
12. Gartrell NK, Milliken N, Goodson WH, Thiemann S, Lo B. Physician-patient sexual contact. Prevalence and problems. West J Med 1992;157:139–143.
13. Carr ML, Robinson GE, Stewart DE, Kussin D. A survey of Canadian psychiatric residents regarding resident-educator sexual contact. Am J Psychiatry 1991;148:216–220.
14. Lamont JA, Woodward C. Patient-physician sexual involvement: a Canadian survey of obstetrician-gynecologists. CMAJ 1994;150:1433–1439.
15. Gallop R. Abuse of power in the nurse-client relationship. Nurs Stand 1998;12:43–47.
16. Rubin SS, Dror O. Professional ethics of psychologists and physicians: morality, confidentiality, and sexuality in Israel. Ethics Behav 1996;6:213–238.
17. Wincze JP, Richards J, Parsons J, Bailey S. A comparative survey of therapist sexual misconduct between an American state and an Australian state. Prof Psychol Res Pr 1996;27:289–294.

18. Foreman S, Stahl M. Chiropractors disciplined by a state chiropractic board and a comparison with disciplined medical physicians. JMPT, September 2004; 27 (7).
19. Morrison J, Wickersham P. Physicians disciplined by a state medical board. JAMA 1998;279:1889–1893.
20. Budnick N. Can't touch this. Willamette Weekly Online, November 27, 2002. Available at: http://www.wweek.com/flatfiles/News3378.lasso. Accessed Month 00, 0000.

How Did We Get Here?
The Social Pendulum

5

In the last five to seven years, society's attitudes about sexual relationships between people in positions of power and those within their control have altered dramatically. The relevance of shifting social opinion to the discussion of professional boundary issues is apparent when one considers that society forms courtroom juries that sit in judgment of professional actions, society provides the patient base in a doctor's practice, and society motivates the development of laws by appealing to their elected representatives for solutions to perceived problems. In short, how society views sexual misconduct has a direct impact on how health-care providers are viewed and judged.

As evidenced by the incidence rates reported in the previous chapter, the number of health-care professionals accused of and disciplined for sexual boundary violations continues to increase. Is this a result solely of regulatory boards becoming more intolerant of such acts? Or is the number of allegations of sexual misconduct rising in direct proportion to the amount of coverage such cases receive in the media?[1] Kroll noted the increasing number of sexual misconduct cases being brought to trial has resulted in additional case law and an expanded notion of what is considered a boundary violation in psychotherapy that "would have been unthinkable 30 to 40 years ago."[2] Kroll added,

> Conspicuously absent in the presentation of guidelines for maintaining proper boundaries ... is some acknowledgment that ... such guidelines are cultural bound, changing every decade or so as new perspectives, economic arrangements, and sociopolitical and risk-management pressures [continue to evolve].

A review of several major events in the United States over the past 10 years suggests a parallel to the increase in the reported incidence of sexual boundary violations among health-care professionals. Since 1991, four major events involving the following people have contributed to rapid swings in the social pendulum: Justice Thomas and Anita Hill, President Clinton and Monica Lewinsky, Mary Kay Letourneau and Vili Fualaau, and Catholic priests and their parishioners. From the details of each event—the accusations against the person in power and the alleged misconduct, ranging from verbal abuse to nonconsensual coital sex—provide a context in which to view sexual boundary issues in the chiropractic profession.

■ Justice Thomas and Anita Hill

In 1991, President George H. Bush nominated Clarence Thomas to the Supreme Court. Thomas had chaired the Equal Employment Opportunity Commission (EEOC) from 1982 through 1990 and was then appointed to the Court of Appeals for the District of Columbia Circuit Court. Shortly after Thomas's appointment went to the Senate floor, Anita Hill, a law professor who had served under Thomas at the EEOC in the 1980s, claimed Thomas had sexually harassed her when she worked for him.[3]

The political storm caused the Senate Judiciary Committee to reopen the appointment hearings, and partisan sides were formed. Hill claimed she was subjected to a hostile work environment marked by Thomas's inappropriate discussions of sexual acts and pornographic films after she rebuffed his invitations to date him. The televised hearings held the public's attention and initiated a public discussion about what constituted sexual harassment, a hostile work environment, and power disparity.

■ Mary Kay Letourneau and Vili Fualaau

Mary Kay Letourneau was a second-grade teacher in Des Moines, Washington, when she first met Vili Fualaau, one of her students. She believed the young Samoan boy was gifted and highly intelligent. Later, after

Letourneau had started teaching fifth and sixth grade classes, Vili Fualaau was once again one of her students. The teacher and student developed a close relationship, with Letourneau confiding in him about her deteriorating marriage, bipolar mental condition, and financial problems.

This increased closeness between teacher and child led to inappropriate behavior and eventually to sexual relations. Police were notified of the relationship on February 25, 1997, when Vili was 13 years of age. Ms. Letourneau became pregnant with her fifth child as a result of her sexual relationship with Vili (the previous four children were from her then-current marriage).

In many states, the statutory rape laws are gender specific, dealing only with adult men who engage in sexual relations with underaged girls. The statutory rape law in Washington, where Ms. Letourneau was employed, is gender neutral and on that basis she was charged with rape of a child. The salacious relationship was front-page material, and a remorseful Ms. Letourneau entered into a plea bargain, which resulted in three months in jail and three years' probation.

Ms. Letourneau ended her jail sentence in January 1998. In February 1998, a police officer making a routine investigation found the former teacher and her student in a parked car, which was a violation of her probation agreement. This time the judge enforced the maximum possible sentence and returned Ms. Letourneau to prison to complete a 7½-year sentence, the maximum for the crime. Shortly after her return to prison, it was determined that she was again pregnant, but the court elected not to pursue a second child rape charge against the former teacher. Letourneau is currently serving out her jail sentence in Washington.

■ President Clinton and Monica Lewinsky

After graduating from college, Monica Lewinsky came to Washington, DC, in June 1995 as an unpaid intern in the White House for Chief of Staff Leon Panetta. Shortly thereafter, she met then-President Clinton, and in November 1995, they began a relationship that included oral sexual relations and sexually explicit telephone conversations. At the end of her internship, Lewinsky moved into a paid position at the Office of Legislative Affairs, which brought her frequently to the

Oval Office. In the spring of 1996, she was transferred to a job in the Pentagon.

During a deposition in a sexual harassment case brought by a former Arkansas state employee, Paula Jones, President Clinton was asked about Monica Lewinsky, who was not involved in the litigation or a public figure at that time. Under oath, President Clinton denied having had sexual relations with Ms. Lewinsky.

Ms. Lewinsky met with federal prosecutors in New York on July 27, 1998, and admitted having had sexual relations with President Clinton. The following day, her lawyers announced a deal for transactional immunity had been reached with the prosecutors. Her subsequent information included her possession of a blue dress that contained DNA information to corroborate her version of events. This highly publicized event created a firestorm around what is considered "sex" as well as what constitutes "ethical" private or public behavior.

■ Priests and Parishioners

John Geoghan, a 67-year-old former priest, stood trial in Boston in December 2001 amid allegations that he had abused 130 children over a 34 year-period.[4] This touched off a scandal of sexual abuse by clergy that had tremendous repercussions. The enormity of the allegations resulted in public shock and demands from the attorney general's office for church records relating to the former priest and others that had similar allegations. Records released in April 2002 revealed not only other priests who had been accused of sexual molestation but also an ongoing pattern of knowledge and cover-ups of incidents by higher church officials. The *Boston Globe* reported the Archdiocese of Boston secretly settled child molestation claims against 70 priests in the past decade.[5] Civil actions were filed by 86 plaintiffs against the Archdiocese of Boston and church supervisors and reached a $10 million settlement.

Pressure from parishioners grew, and polls in the *Boston Globe* showed that approximately 50% of Boston's Catholics demanded accountability from church officials, specifically, the resignation of Cardinal Bernard Law. The Catholic Cardinals of the United States met and adopted a zero-tolerance policy toward clergy abuse, but damage from the scandal continued to mount. After that time, the scandal spread to other cities, and other priests were accused of abuse.

■ Impact of Social Events on Issues of Doctor-Patient Relationships

The four cases have resulted in producing a major shift in societal attitudes regarding improper relationships between people in positions of power and those over whom they assume that power. The examples also identify the scope of sexual allegations—from verbal sexual harassment (Anita Hill) to oral sex (Monica Lewinsky).

As former Secretary of State Henry Kissinger once observed, "power is a great aphrodisiac." One would have to wonder if Monica Lewinsky, a "consenting adult," would have been quite as enamored with Bill Clinton if he had been a small-town used car salesman instead of the most powerful man on the earth. With the recent media attention on this subject, the public has elevated expectations regarding the ethical behavior of anyone in a position of authority and power. Given that the doctor-patient relationship is one of the strongest of all fiduciary relationships (as discussed in Chapter 6), it is not surprising to see the incidence rate of reported misconduct mentioned earlier in this work parallel the social events that have occurred in the previous decade. This has prompted some to contemplate a complete ban on male doctors treating women. Pollack poses the question, "Should men treat women?" and then replies, "With some restraint, I answer yes, but only if they are sensitive and empathic to normative developmental needs of women."[6]

Endnotes

1. Szabo CP, Kohn R, Gordon A, Levav I, Hart GA. Ethics in the practice of psychiatry in South Africa. S Afr Med J 2000;90:498–503.
2. Kroll J. Boundary violations: a cultural-bound syndrome. J Am Acad Psychiatry Law 2001;29:274–282.
3. Lewis NA. Law professor accuses Thomas of sexual harassment in 1980s. New York Times, October.7, 1991.
4. Burge K. Teen declines to testify, so DA drops one case against Geoghan. Boston Globe, November 14, 2002.
5. Farragher T. Admission of awareness damning for law. Boston Globe, December 14, 2002.
6. Pollack WS. Should men treat women? Dilemmas for the male psychotherapist: psychoanalytic and developmental perspectives. Ethics Behav 1992;2:39–49.

Absolute Morality and Zero Tolerance

6

The zero-tolerance policies regarding weapons and drugs implemented in many public schools across the United States are deeply rooted in the principles of absolute morality. Despite what appears to be a logical consistency in arguing for an absolute morality, the argument is intellectually dishonest and its support specious. In fact, it is extremely difficult to apply an absolute standard to most human behaviors, as the propriety of any human action is usually conditional. For example, consider the act of stealing, which is almost always viewed as illegal. Almost everyone would agree that it is immoral to steal an item of value from another person. The item of value may be a purse, a car, or the design plans for a competitor's product. As long as there is value in the item being stolen, stealing is logically judged wrong. Thus, using linear logic, all forms of stealing should be punished in the same manner.

■ Penalties and Punishments

What if your job is to steal information from terrorists who are planning a nuclear attack on New York City? By definition, this is also stealing. From an absolute standard of morality, the person "stealing" information from others should be judged and punished in the same manner as the thief who steals an elderly man's wallet at gunpoint. No mitigating factors should be considered. No discussion of intent can be made using such standards. In essence, there are no gray areas when dealing with absolute morality. The algorithm of absolute morality is linear, with no branches in the decision-making process.

However, life is rarely without ambiguity. The application of absolute morality is exactly how fourth-grade boys using "finger guns" are logically judged to have breached the same ethical standards as those who have brought real guns to school.

When dealing with many ethical issues, including the issues surrounding professional boundaries, it is dangerous and intellectually naïve to use such rigid standards. In fact, an absolute morality can be quite dangerous. Some proponents of the zero-tolerance principles of absolute morality would require all who commit sexual misdeeds to register as sex offenders, not just those found guilty of criminal conduct (which demands a great deal of evidence).[1] Under an absolute morality, situational facts are irrelevant. A health-care professional who admits to telling an inappropriate sexual joke would be guilty of the lowest form of sexual misconduct and be required to register as a sex offender. While some would consider such a proposition to be hyperbole, who would have thought a 5-year-old would be suspended from kindergarten for bringing a plastic ax to school on Halloween? Is it reasonable to put a college student involved in a streaking prank in the same category as a registered sex offender? Although clearly the college student was naked in front of the public, should his act be judged the same as that of the man who exposes his genitals in public for sexual gratification? How significant are the differences in the two men's intentions? The rigid standards of absolute morality do not allow for the consideration of intent.

The movement to register all sex offenders appears to be gaining momentum. Recall that in the early 1990s, Searight and Campbell observed that sex-offender laws reflected the mood of the public and elected officials.[2] Although their observation could be considered an example of legal hyperbole, the recent media attention given to the scandals within the Catholic Church suggest that we might expect to see more efforts to expand the definition of unprofessional conduct as well as the penalties of such conduct. The prudent registration of those found guilty of a sexual offense in criminal court is a laudable undertaking, but the same cannot be said for the registration of those found guilty of sexual misconduct in tribunals using lower forms of evidence (i.e., preponderance of evidence and clear and convincing evidence; see Chapter 11). These lower courts must weigh the issues and intent of the accused before considering the strict remedies mandated by higher courts.

■ Fiduciary Relationships

The honor and elevated social status conferred on health-care providers are well established in almost all societies. In the Far East as well as among the Native Americans of North America, those who aid others are typically placed at the highest levels of social standing. For most people in Western society, the word *doctor* evokes positive connotations with educational achievement and wisdom. This public perception of health-care providers is largely a result of the intimate nature of the doctor-patient relationship. Both individual patients and society as a whole value the doctor-patient relationship as sacred. Consequently, with the elevated social status and financial rewards of health-care professions come public responsibilities. Legislators as well as the public expect health-care providers to conform to the highest moral standards. People need to be able to know and trust their health-care providers.

Patients should have the comfort of knowing that nothing they say to their doctors will result in social or political judgment. Without such trust in the doctor-patient relationship, patients are likely to omit certain social or historical facts that could affect their care and treatment. For example, a 28-year-old homosexual male who has contracted AIDS must feel assured that his health-care providers are not going to treat his condition differently because of his sexual orientation. If the man denies engaging in unprotected sexual contact or using needles, other sources of the disease would have to be identified for the public's protection. The man's dentist could have spread the disease to his patient population, or there might be a problem with the blood supply used in transfusions.

The fiduciary relationship lies at the core of public trust. The term *fiduciary* is derived from Latin and means "give faithful service."[3] The fiduciary relationship requires the doctor to make decisions that are in the best interest of the patient, not the doctor. No factors should interfere with the doctor making the best, most unbiased, decisions on behalf of the patient. To eliminate any factors that could contaminate the doctor-patient relationship, the fiduciary is required to relinquish all personal interests for the sake of what is best for the patient. In other words, patients must be able to trust that their doctors are making decisions that are not contaminated by self-serving motives and represent the most prudent clinical course. For example, a patient should have complete trust that a doctor is performing a surgery because that is the correct clinical course, rather than to secure money to buy a new car. Performing a surgery for monetary gain, as opposed to the needs of the patient, would represent a breach in the fiduciary responsibilities of the doctor.

Clearly, the fact that a patient is frequently at the mercy of the doctor's decision-making skill yields an inequity in the distribution of power in the doctor-patient relationship. The requirements of a fiduciary put the doctor in a special position of power over the patient. An unethical surgeon has the ability, and more importantly the power, to convince a patient that unnecessary tests and surgery may be needed. It is unreasonable to expect that a patient would have the medical knowledge necessary to decide if the doctor is, in fact, telling the truth about the need for surgery. That is why the fiduciary relationship is so essential in the delivery of health care. Before meeting with any health-care provider, a patient must know that the doctor is using sound clinical judgment on the patient's behalf. The public, too, must know that all decisions being made are not contaminated, in any way, by motives that are less than clinical. The proper professional doctor-patient relationship is secured by a reliable set of professional boundaries, on which the patient, the doctor, the public, and legislators can depend.

A fiduciary relationship is established with each doctor-patient relationship, no matter the profession, specialty, or geographic location. The relationship is not bound by any formal agreement; it is inherent in every doctor-patient relationship. The special trust that a patient places in the hands of a health-care provider is truly the basis of the elevated status that society places in those who dedicate their lives to helping others.

A "dual relationship" occurs when a health-care provider is placed in the situation to split allegiances between the doctor-patient relationship and other non-clinical relationships. Pope suggested reasons why dual relationships are problematic.[4]

1. The dual relationship erodes and distorts the professional nature of the therapeutic relationship.
2. Dual relationships create conflicts of interest.
3. Either during the course of care or after care has ended, the therapist may be compelled to offer testimony regarding the patient's diagnosis, treatment, and prognosis. Such testimony would become suspect.

4. If dual relationships were deemed acceptable, therapists could use their practice as a dating service, culling out patients who are truly in need to meet their own social, sexual, or financial agendas.

It is interesting to note that Pope considered even nonsexual dual relationships (landlord, best friend, and employer) in the same category as sexual dual relationships.

Endnotes

1. Rutter P. Sex in the Forbidden Zone. London: Unwin Press, 1992.
2. Searight HR, Campbell DC. Physician-patient sexual contact: ethical and legal issues and clinical guidelines. J Fam Pract 1993;36:647–653.
3. Gutheil TG. Ethical issues in sexual misconduct by clinicians. Jpn J Psychiatry Neurol 1994;48(Suppl):39–44.
4. Pope KS. Dual relationships in psychotherapy. Ethics Behav 1991;1:21–34.

Power Within the Doctor-Patient Relationship

7

The power and influence derived from a doctor-patient relationship differ among specialties. For example, the field of behavioral sciences encompasses many provider types with a wide range of training and clinical management roles. At one end of the spectrum are social workers and marriage and family counselors. These practitioners do not typically deal with patients who are housed in psychiatric residences, nor do they have the training or license required to prescribe medications. At the other end of the spectrum are psychologists and medically trained psychiatrists. Because they deal with more serious forms of mental illnesses, these practitioners wield greater power and influence over their patients than do other professionals in the field.

Table 7-1 summarizes the level of involvement of specialties in the treatment of patients. The first category, paraprofessionals, comprises nurses and other licensed health-care providers who are involved in the treatment of patients with many different types of diseases and in a multitude of clinical settings—in a doctor's office (outpatient), in a hospital (inpatient), or in a long-term care facility (residential setting).

In the behavioral sciences, doctors are divided into two basic categories, strictly based on licensing and the mode of treatment dictated by each license. A psychiatrist, who holds a medical degree and a plenary license (i.e., unlimited in terms of scope of practice, has the training and expertise to prescribe medications and, if necessary, to perform surgery (e.g., lobotomies). A psychologist, who typically has a Ph.D. rather than a medical degree, provides care via counseling. The allopathic category represents all medical practitioners who do not treat the mentally ill as their primary vocation. The breadth of the category is extremely wide, ranging from neurologists to podiatrists. Representing the nonplenary

TABLE 7-1 ■ TYPES OF CARE PROVIDED BY HEALTH-CARE PROFESSIONALS

| PROVIDER TYPE | PRACTICE SETTING | | | AUTHORITY TO | | | LEVEL OF MEDICAL DECISION MAKING |
	OUTPATIENT	INPATIENT	RESIDENTIAL	PRESCRIBE DRUGS	ADMINISTER ANESTHESIA	TREAT MENTAL ILLNESS	
Paraprofessional	Yes	Yes	Maybe	No	No	Yes	Low
Behavioral—MD	Yes	Yes	Yes	Yes	Yes	Yes	Low to High
Behavioral—Non-MD	Yes	Yes	Yes	No	No	Yes	Low to High
Allopathic	Yes	Yes	Yes	Yes	Yes	No	Low to High
Chiropractic	Yes	No	No	No	No	No	Low to Moderate

category of licensure is the chiropractic profession. A nonplenary license is restricted in terms of the legally allowed treatments and scope of practice.

The column headings in Table 7-1 represent the various types of care that health-care providers offer. While each specialty includes a small group that would contradict these categorizations, the table reflects a commonsense, generalized view. For instance, although some chiropractors perform manipulations under anesthesia, anecdotally this appears to be a very small proportion of the approximately 66,790 chiropractors practicing in the United States.[1]

All listed health-care professionals provide care to patients on an outpatient basis, and except for chiropractors, generally all provide care on an inpatient basis. Patients requiring inpatient care on a long-term basis—such as elderly or chronically ill patients, those recovering from surgery or receiving treatment in hospice settings, or those either temporarily or permanently housed in psychiatric facilities—may receive their care from any of the health-care professions listed in the table, with the exception of the chiropractors.

Only licensed physicians (both behavioral and allopathic) can prescribe medication in the treatment of disease. For the sake of discussion, this category also includes the hybrid vocations of nurse practitioners and physician assistants.

Although health-care providers of all types deal with mild forms of mental illness on a daily basis, the professionals who care for patients with moderate to severe forms of conditions such as depression, psychoses, and bipolar disorders are almost exclusively in the behavioral sciences.

The final category that helps define the power derived from the doctor-patient relationship is the type of medical decisions made by the providers. The table reflects the medical decision-making guidelines provided in the evaluation and management section of the American Medical Association's Current Procedural Terminology. The level of medical decision making ranges from low to high. An office visit with a family practitioner for the removal of sutures would represent straightforward medical decision making for a condition with low morbidity and/or mortality. On the other hand, a consultation with an oncologist for treatment of breast cancer represents highly complex medical decision making; the oncologist must use a great deal of clinical acumen on behalf of the patient. Likewise, professionals in the behavioral sciences who care for patients with suicidal ideologies are required to make decisions regarding use of restraints and medications and allowing interactions with other in-patient residents; these are also highly complex medical decisions. With some exceptions, the chiropractic license as well as the type of therapy administered, typified by outpatient care, does not require complex medical decision making.

A review of the findings shown in Table 7-1 reveals that the chiropractic profession is unique among the health-care specialties. Generally, the chiropractic profession does not administer care in hospital or residential settings. Chiropractic manipulative therapy is not typically administered to patients who are in an unconscious state, nor does it require medication. Certainly, chiropractic manipulative therapy is not a form of treatment for those who suffer from mental illness. Chiropractors treat patients on an outpatient basis and typically do not have contact with patients in residential settings, nor do they deal with patients who have moderate to severe forms of mental illnesses. Because of their training, licensing, the type of therapy they administer, and the type of conditions they treat, chiropractors do not work with a high probability of morbidity or mortality.

Given the uniqueness of the chiropractic profession, the power and potential influence of chiropractors over their patients are less than those of the other health-care providers. This should not be interpreted as meaning that the chiropractic professional has a lower clinical standing than the medical practitioner or the behavioral scientist. Simply, as Table 7-1 shows, there is a spectrum of power derived from the various specialties, thus doctor-patient relationships have various distributions of power or potential influence.

The doctor-patient relationship is one of several fiduciary relationships—for instance, attorney-client, banker-depositor, and teacher-student. Are these other fiduciary relationships under the same obligations as the doctor-patient relationship, which is often thought to represent the prototypical fiduciary relationship? It would be irrational to expect a banker to abstain from dating a former client for 2 years after all the client's financial dealings with the bank had ended. Clearly, society has established different power paradigms for different types of fiduciary relationships. Is it any less reasonable to assume that different health-care providers wield different levels of power over their patients? Or are all doctor-patient relationships equal in all ways? It is the differences between the professions that argue against a single standard to judge the propriety of conduct.

Some individuals might argue that the idea that differences exist between the chiropractic and medical professions, even in the context of doctor-patient relationships, reduces the chiropractic profession to a role secondary to that of the medical professions. However, this argument is incorrect. This is not a chiropractic-versus-medical issue. Power differences exist among specialties within the medical profession itself. For example, obstetricians and gynecologists contend that they have a higher level of fiduciary relationship, and therefore power, than do other medical specialties. In November 1994, the American College of Obstetricians and Gynecologists articulated the degree of specialty status they have with their patients compared with other medical specialties:

> The obstetrician-gynecologist may fill many roles of patients: as primary physician, technology expert, prevention specialist, counselor, and confidante. Privy to both birth and death, obstetrician-gynecologists assist women as they pass through adolescence; grow into maturity; make choices about sexuality, partnership, and family; experience the sorrows of reproductive loss, infertility, and illness; and adapt to the transitions of midlife and aging. The practice of obstetrics and gynecology includes interaction at times of intense emotion and vulnerability for the patient and involves both sensitive physical examination and medically necessary disclosure of especially private information about symptoms and experiences.

The special doctor-patient relationship of OB/Gyn's and their associated power carries the burden of a higher standard of ethical conduct. Likewise, health-care providers whose patients are facing life-and-death situations must command a high level of trust from their patients. It is not hard to understand that a patient facing a heart transplant would have a higher degree of trust in the cardiologist than a patient receiving treatments for spinal fixations on a maintenance basis would have in the chiropractor.

Discussions of issues surrounding sexual misconduct are directly related to the issues of power derived from the doctor-patient relationship. We argue strongly that doctors of chiropractic should not be held to the same power and influence standards of other health-care providers, whose licensure and treatment bring with it a far more intimate level of emotional and physical contact.

Endnotes

1. Smith M, Carber L. Chiropractic health care in health professional shortage areas in the United States. Am J Public Health 2002;92:2001–2009.

Transference and Countertransference

8

A complete understanding of the power associated with fiduciary relationships requires insight into transference and countertransference.
Transference is the unconscious assignment of feelings and attitudes of
important figures in the past to persons in the present.[1] *Countertransference* occurs when a therapist transfers emotions and/or feelings to
the patient. Both terms encompass strong emotions that can play a
significant role in defining a doctor-patient relationship.

As trust develops between a patient and a doctor, most notably a
psychotherapist, the patient might unconsciously misinterpret the doctor's role. The patient might view the health-care provider as a parent—a
protector and caretaker—reflecting the patient's memories or perceptions of his or her own parent. Likening the doctor-patient relationship
to the parent-child relationship, along with applying an absolute morality, has led to the notion that doctor-patient sexual misconduct is the
moral equivalent of incest. One proponent of this analogy was Brodsky,
who argued as follows:

> A therapist is a therapist for life, just as a parent is a parent for life, no matter
> how the quantity or quality of that relationship changes over time. . . . No
> matter how the therapy contract ends, the imbalance of power of the initial
> interactions can never be erased. Thus, therapists need to agree that once
> they accept a patient into therapy, that patient becomes off limits to any
> other relationship. The patient needs to know that the relationship is safe.[2]

The mere fact that an adult patient would seek care places the
patient in a childlike position of vulnerability. Some therapists argue that transference—the patient seeing the therapist as a parental

figure—must occur for the psychotherapy to be effective.[3] This statement implies that the level of trust, and therefore power, within the therapist-patient relationship has to be extremely high for effective treatment to occur. Gutheil expanded on this idea, saying, "I subscribe to the notion that transference is universal and found to a greater or lesser degree in all human relationships."[4]

The following are some common themes in patient transference[5]:

- Dr. Perfect (idealization)
- Dr. Prince Charming (romantic idol, rescue)
- Dr. Good Parent (nurturing, reparenting)
- Dr. Magical Healer (savior)
- Dr. Beneficent (devoted caretaker, e.g., nanny or childhood doctor)
- Dr. Indispensable (only one who can cure)
- Dr. Omniscient (knows and understands all)

In terms of chiropractic care, a review of the literature failed to uncover any contributions on this subject. As a result, the profession is vulnerable to adopting professional standards of care that incorporate transference attitudes like those listed. As a provider of complementary or alternative medicine, the chiropractor may be **more** likely than other health-care providers to be the subject of the common themes just listed. Many patients enter complementary or alternative care because they believe its practitioners have a better listening ear to the subjective complaints of patients. Does the chiropractic profession thus foster the notion of being "Dr. Indispensable" or "Dr. Good Parent?"

■ Countertransference

While some degree of countertransference is often necessary in the doctor-patient relationship, erotic countertransference most often leads to mismanagement of the patient.[6,7] Pope et al. surveyed 575 psychotherapists and found that 95% of male and 76% of female psychotherapists felt sexually attracted to their clients and that 9.4% of the men and 2.5% of the women acted on those feelings.[8] Extrapolating to other health-care specialties, it would seem naïve to conclude that only those involved in psychotherapy would have such feelings for their patients. In fact, the reported incidence rates of sexual misconduct among other health-care professions and the number of disciplinary actions taken by their regulatory boards demonstrate that few health-care providers act on their sexual feelings towards their patients.

Given the paucity of writing on this subject in relation to the chiropractic profession, it is unknown if practitioners thought to provide complementary or alternative medicine are more susceptible to issues of countertransference.

Endnotes

1. Simon RI. Sexual misconduct of therapists: a cause for civil and criminal action. Trial 1985;21:46–51.
2. Brodsky AM. Sex between therapists and patients: ethical gray area. Psychotherapy in Private Practice 1985;3:57–62.
3. Kardener S. Sex and the physician-patient relationship. Am J Psychiatry 1974;131: 1134–1136.
4. Gutheil TG. Ethical issues in sexual misconduct by clinicians. Jpn J Psychiatry Neurol 1994;48(Suppl):39–44.
5. Simon RI. Therapist-patient sex: from boundary violations to sexual misconduct. Psychiatr Clin North Am 1999;22:31–47.
6. Winnecott D. Hate in the countertransference. Int J Psychoanal 1949;30:69–75.
7. Simon RI. Therapist-patient sex: from boundary violations to sexual misconduct. Psychiatr Clin North Am 1999;22:31–47.
8. Pope KS, Keithe-Speigel P, Tabachneck BG. Sexual attraction to clients. The human therapist and the (sometimes) inhuman training system. Am Psychol 1986;41:147–158.

The Slippery Slope

9

A review of the literature reveals that sexual abuse by health-care professionals can be categorized into groups based on when the abuse occurs. In one category is the abuse of patients at the first meeting. Such abuse includes molesting patients while under anesthesia, videotaping patients while gowning,[1] and examining patients' genitalia under false clinical pretense during the initial examination, to name a few. The other category comprises long-term patient abuse. Over time, the doctor-patient relationship slowly erodes and may subtly evolve into the most serious type of abuse, sexual intercourse between doctor and patient.[2,3] The term *slippery slope* has been used to describe the slow deterioration of the practitioner's fiduciary responsibilities.[4]

■ The Transition Zone

The behavioral sciences have identified an area in which the slippery slope is most likely to occur—the physical space between the time the patient leaves the "chair" and the time the patient exits the therapist's office. This space is called the transition zone.[5] In the chiropractic office, the transition zone is the area from the table to the door. One of the most interesting elements of the transition zone is the patient dialogue that occurs there. In describing what he called exit lines, Gabbard noted that it "may be the most important communication of the hour, conveying a message that the patient feels he cannot say on the couch or the chair."[6] Thus, careful attention to the statements patients make in the transition zone could provide the greatest insight into possible issues of transference.

Likewise, the remarks a practitioner makes in the transition zone can affect the doctor-patient relationship. A patient conflicted by transference issues might misinterpret a final comment of "I want to see you three times next week" or "I can't wait to see you next week to see how far we can progress." The patient could interpret either comment to mean the doctor wants to establish and develop a personal relationship. All clinicians should be aware of the heightened potential for misunderstanding within the transition zone.

In psychotherapy, the transition zone has been described as the most opportune location for crossing physical boundaries. As an area of increased physical proximity between patient and therapist, the transition zone provides the opportunity for accidental or purposeful touching. Even a seemingly benign hug might be interpreted in profoundly different ways as was pointed out in the Introduction.[7]

Various actions along the slippery slope can lead to sexual misconduct. Simon described the development of a sexual relationship between therapist and patient as a progression of at least some of the following boundary violations:[8]

1. Gradually allowing neutrality to erode.
2. Socializing therapy.
3. Treating patient as "special."
4. Disclosing confidential information about other patients.
5. Self-disclosing.
6. Initiating physical contact (e.g., touching, hugging, kissing).
7. Gaining control over the patient.
8. Initiating extratherapeutic contacts.
9. Extending length of therapy sessions.
10. Scheduling therapy sessions at the end of the day.
11. Ceasing to bill patient.
12. Dating patient.
13. Initiating sexual intercourse.

Robinson and Stewart came up with a very similar list of warning signs that a physician is on the edge of the professional boundary:[9]

- Intrusive thoughts of the patient
- Feelings of falling in love with the patient

- Arranging appointments with the patient for times when other staff have left the office
- Thoughts of meeting the patient outside the office
- According "special" treatment to the patient
- Making increasingly irrelevant self-disclosures to the patient
- Acting in a way the physician would not want colleagues to know about

Both lists suggest that the initial visit between doctor and patient does not provide sufficient time to cross several of the lesser boundary violations. The power a doctor holds in the relationship is also developed over time. Hypothetically, if an initial doctor-patient encounter produced a mutual "love at first sight" that prompted an immediate termination of the doctor-patient relationship, the disproportionate power inherent in the doctor-patient relationship would need to be appropriately weighed.

Another factor that determines the level of power a doctor has over a patient and the progression of physical boundary violations is the number of patient visits. Once again, it is hard to imagine that many of the actions in the preceding two lists could occur over a span of just three to six office visits.

■ Spectrum of Sexual Misconduct

The prohibition against sexual relationships between doctors and their patients dates back to Hippocrates. The Hippocratic oath is still taken by medicals physicians upon graduation from medical schools across the world and is the basis of most health-care providers ethical code of conduct. The list of what is considered to be sexual misconduct has lengthened since the time of Hippocrates to include acts ranging from sexual innuendo to coitus. Summer and McCrory identified 10 sexual offenses that reveal the breadth of the spectrum:[10]

1. Affairs with vulnerable patients.
2. Inappropriate sexual touching through massage or masturbation.
3. Inappropriate affectionate behavior (kissing and hugging).

4. Unnecessary sexual talk with patients (talking about irrelevant sexual conduct, orgasms, masturbation).
5. Exposing patients.
6. Forcible rape of patients.
7. Taking pictures of patients for sexual purposes.
8. Peeping on patients undressing.
9. Using vulnerable patients to gain sexual access to their children.
10. Sexual involvement with staff or residents that they supervise.

By including sexual exploitation with sexual misconduct, Jones and Adkins add to the spectrum of what is considered inappropriate behavior by health-care providers:[11]

1. Inappropriate touching.
2. Sexually exploitative relationships that may occur during or after a formal professional relationship.
3. "Therapeutic" sexual acts, which are sexual acts a health-care practitioner claims will benefit the patient but actually are meant for the practitioner's own stimulation.
4. Sexual assault of sedated and unconscious patients.

■ Terminology

The terms *sexual misconduct* and *professional boundary* are frequently used side-by-side in the literature. These terms are also used in the context of other fiduciary relationships, including attorney-client, teacher-student, banker-depositor, or minister-parishioner relationships. The term *sexual harassment* is associated with allegations that arise in the workplace. Although sexual harassment and sexual misconduct typically parallel one another socially and legally, they are distinctly different.

A *professional boundary* can be defined as the clinical distance and respect afforded a patient who receives care from a health-care provider. Certainly, what constitutes a "reasonable and ethical distance" and "respect" is open to interpretation. As is often the case in any discussion of human actions, different actions can mean different things to different people.

An example of such disagreement involves the simple act of hugging. Some patients would find such physical contact with a doctor to be offensive, while others would view a hug as a warm display of "bedside manner." Others might view the rejection of a hug as cultural insensitivity.[12] Gartrell included hugging as sexual contact if the physical contact "arouses or satisfies sexual desire."[13] Even patients who are not offended by a single hug might believe that a hug at every visit is an attempt to advance to an erotic relationship. Other patients may not object to the number of hugs but are made uncomfortable by the duration of each embrace. Again, it is a subjective assessment.

Strictly speaking, the physical contact of a hug between a doctor and a patient does not have a quantifiable clinical value. No disease is treated by hugging. However, it would be almost inconceivable to any sympathetic practitioner not to give a hug to a patient who, for instance, has just been diagnosed with end-stage cancer. Gutheil and Gabbard found that most physicians working with HIV and AIDS patients want to touch their patients in a benign manner (e.g., a gentle pat on the back or squeeze of an arm) on each visit to keep patients from feeling "like lepers."[14] Despite the good intentions of these physicians, zero-tolerance standards would dictate that a hug be considered a breach of the proper amount of clinical distance between a doctor and patient.

Sheets compiled the work of Peterson and Simon to establish levels of professional boundaries that specifically address the concerns of the nursing profession. Sheets also identified three classifications of sexual misconduct:[15]

1. **Boundary crossing:** a brief excursion across professional boundaries followed by a return to established limits of the professional relationship.
2. **Boundary violation:** a breach of professional boundaries in which the practitioner sets personal needs above those of the patient.
3. **Professional sexual misconduct:** a breach of trust. As Sheets states, "Any behavior by a nurse that is seductive, sexually demeaning, harassing or reasonably interpreted by a client as sexual, is a violation of the nurse's fiduciary responsibility to the client." Sexual acts with a patient who has given consent are still considered sexual misconduct.

Although these various definitions provide some clarity to the issues surrounding sexual misconduct and professional boundaries, many questions remain. For example, what is sex? When asked that question during his testimony before the grand jury regarding his relationship with Monica Lewinsky, President Clinton made the now-famous declaration, "It depends on what the meaning of the word *is* is." More to the point, Simon defined *sexual activity* to include intercourse, rape, the touching of breasts and genitals, cunnilingus, fellatio, sodomy, and inappropriate or unnecessary examination and procedures for sexual gratification.[16]

■ Statements from Organizations

Several organizations worldwide have attempted to bring clarity to this subject of sexual misconduct and professional misconduct. The Medical Council of New Zealand divided the topic of sexual misconduct into three categories:[17]

1. Sexual impropriety
2. Sexual transgression
3. Sexual violation

The council defined a sexual impropriety as the lowest level of misconduct, which refers to inappropriate nonphysical actions by the doctor that the patient considers "disrespectful in manner and sexually demeaning." Examples include inappropriate jokes, crude gestures, or even demeaning comments about a patient's undergarments.

A sexual transgression involves inappropriate physical contact between the doctor and the patient, stopping short of an overt sexual act. This includes a doctor examining a patient's erogenous zones under false clinical pretenses and performing pelvic examinations without gloves.

The most egregious category, the sexual violation, involves a sexual act between doctor and patient and is not limited solely to coital contact. The council included genital intercourse, oral sex, anal intercourse, and mutual masturbation as examples of sex acts.

Similar to the Medical Council of New Zealand, the College of Physicians and Surgeons of Alberta, Canada have defined three levels of sexual abuse: sexual impropriety, sexual violation level I, and sexual violation level II.[18] An example of a sexual impropriety is "a remark made by a gynecologist to a woman during her examination 6 weeks after the birth of her first child: 'That's nice and tight. I bet your husband is a happy man.'" Other examples of nonphysical sexual impropriety are a doctor initiating a conversation about personal sexual problems, preferences, or fantasies and asking to date the patient.[19]

Examination of genitalia, breasts, or anus under false clinical pretense were given as examples of a level-I sexual violation. The most serious level of abuse defined by the Canadian organization is a level-II sexual violation, which is sexual intercourse between doctor and patient.

The standards of both the Medical Council of New Zealand and the College of Physicians and Surgeons of Alberta, Canada do not specify whether the standards are to apply to both current and former doctor-patient relationships.

Endnotes

1. Board of Chiropractic Examiners State of California, Accusation No. 1993-13.
2. A case of professional sexual misconduct. N C Med J 1996;57:208–212.
3. Gutheil TG, Gabbard GO. The concept of boundaries in clinical practice: theoretical and risk-management dimensions. Am J Psychiatry 1993;150:188–196.
4. Strasburger LJ, Jorgenson L, Sutherland P. The prevention of psychotherapist sexual misconduct: avoiding the slippery slope. Am J Psychother 1992;46:544–554.
5. Gutheil TG, Simon TI. Between the chair and the door: boundary issues in the therapeutic "transition zone." Harvard Rev Psychiatry 1995;2:336–340.
6. Gabbard GO. The exit lines are said to be the time when heightened transference-counter-transference manifestations occur. J Am Psychoanal Assoc 1982;30:579–598.
7. Gutheil TG, Simon TI. Harvard Rev Psychiatry 1995;2:336–340.
8. Simon RI. Therapist-patient sex: from boundary violations to sexual misconduct. Psychiatr Clin North Am 1999;22:31–47.
9. Robinson GE, Stewart DE. A curriculum on physician-patient sexual misconduct and teacher-learner mistreatment. Part 2: teaching method. CMAJ 1996;154:1021–1025.
10. Summer GL, McCrory E. Professional sexual misconduct: the current reality, current concepts, ignorance is no excuse. Ala Med 1994;64:4–6.
11. Jones LE, Adkins E. Allegations of sexual misconduct: a risk management perspective. J Healthc Risk Manag 1997;17:8–14.
12. White GE, Coverdale JA, Thomson AN. Can one be a good doctor and have a sexual relationship with one's patient? Fam Pract 1994;11:389–393.
13. Gartrell NK, Milliken N, Goodson WH, Thiemann S, Lo B. Physician-patient sexual contact: prevalence and problems. West J Med 1992;157:139–143.
14. Gutheil TG, Gabbard GO. Am J Psychiatry 1993;150:188–196.

15. College of Physicians and Surgeons of Ontario. Task force on sexual abuse of patients 1993.
16. Sheets VR. Raising awareness regarding the phenomenon of professional sexual misconduct. Dean' s Notes 1996;18:1–2.
17. Simon RI. Therapist-patient sex: from boundary violations to sexual misconduct. Psychiatr Clin North Am 1999;22:31–47.
18. Medical Council of New Zealand. Sexual abuse in the doctor-patient relationship: discussion document for the profession. Newslett Med. Council N.Z. 1992;6:4–5.
19. Sullivan P. Alberta committee on sexual exploitation demands tough penalties for abusers. CMAJ 1992;147:934.

10

Sexual Relationships with Current and Former Patients

Ethical issues are rarely black and white, especially when dealing with human sexual activities. Nevertheless, current literature shows that there's little ambiguity when it comes to the ethics of doctors having sexual relations with their patients. There is nearly universal agreement from all corners of the world that a doctor must be prohibited from having sexual relations with a current patient. Often, however, the statutes or codes of ethics that make this prohibition fail to define key terms, leaving the rules open to wide interpretation. The issue of sexual contact between doctor and former patients has not received widespread attention and is similarly steeped in ambiguity.

■ Current Patients

Regulations Adopted by Organizations Worldwide

The following is a summary of the regulations established by various groups across the globe on the subject of sexual contact concurrent with an ongoing doctor-patient relationship.

- American Medical Association, Council on Ethical and Judicial Affairs, 1991: "Sexual contact or a romantic relationship with a patient concurrent with a physician-patient relationship is unethical."[1]
- American College of Obstetricians and Gynecologists, Committee on Ethics: Endorsed the AMA position as well as the

position of the Society of Obstetricians and Gynecologists of Canada, which stated in 1992, "Sexual contact or a romantic relationship between a physician and a current patient is always unethical."[2]

- American Psychiatry Association, 1994: "Sexual activity with a current or a former patient is unethical."[3]
- Canadian Medical Association, 1994: "Physicians should never be sexually or romantically involved with their current patients."[4]
- Canadian Psychiatric Association, 1989: "Eroticizing the physician/patient relationship is unacceptable under any circumstances and cannot be rationalized as therapy."[5]
- Royal Australian and New Zealand College of Psychiatrists, 1990: "Sexual relationships between psychiatrists and their patients are always unethical."[6]
- Florida, state law regulating the practice of dentistry, 1992: "Sexual misconduct. The dentist-patient relationship is founded on mutual trust. Sexual misconduct in the practice of dentistry means violation of the dentist-patient relationship.... Sexual misconduct in the practice of dentistry is prohibited."[7]
- West Virginia Board of Medicine, 1993: "The rules of the West Virginia Board of Medicine state that it is unprofessional conduct to fail to conform to the principles of the medical ethics of the American Medical Association."[8]

The ethical standards and the laws in England governing the issues surrounding sexual misconduct parallel those seen in the United States. In fact, after reviewing the laws and ethical standards of psychotherapist organizations around the world (United States, England, Canada, Australia, New Zealand, Israel, Saudi Arabia, Kuwait, Norway, Sweden, Finland, West Germany, Brazil, and Mexico), Coleman concluded, "Virtually universal condemnation exists for sexual contact between therapist and patient."[9]

In terms of penalties for admitted sexual misconduct on behalf of the therapist, Arabian countries having strong Islamic legal derivations had the most serious repercussions: "If the doctor is not married, he will be flogged 100 times and will be permanently dismissed from his job. The married therapist will be killed if he confesses or if the sexual act was seen by four witnesses."[10]

With such a consensus, the issue of having sexual relations during an extant doctor-patient relationship appears to be unequivocal.

However, a number of issues blur the lines of this supposed black-and-white issue. Some will argue that prohibiting any consensual sexual relationship is in direct conflict with the rights afforded to the American public under the due process clause in the U.S. Constitution and state constitutions.[11] Yet to be tested is the question of whether a person's right to freely choose sexual partners is superseded by his or her professional obligations.

Ambiguous Regulatory Language

Many of the statements made by the various organizations are so vague that they are rendered useless under the light of scrutiny. For example, the AMA's position that "sexual contact or a romantic relationship" is unethical is not supported by clearly defined terms. As discussed in Chapter 9, there is a great deal of debate about the definition of *sex* and what is considered inappropriate touching under false clinical pretenses. Trying to define the elements of a "romantic relationship" brings up many questions. Is sending flowers to a patient a "romantic relationship"? What about calling the patient after hours? Should a hug or holding hands be seen as romantic advances? If so, when does such behavior constitute a "relationship"? In our review of the literature, we found no definition of *romantic relationship*. Given the often severe penalties associated with violating sexual misconduct standards, the lack of meaningful and legally enforceable definitions leaves any attempt to categorize human conduct in such absolute terms fraught with frailties. The legal transparency of such definitions led Simon to conclude, "Statutory definitions of sexual misconduct cannot encompass the wide variety of sexual activities that constitute the abuse of patients by therapists."[12]

Regulations in the Rural Practice

How does the health-care provider who practices in a rural setting deal with such strict standards? The attitudes of rural providers concerning potential sexual contact were considered in a Canadian survey that found physicians in small communities were three times more likely to approve of asking a patient for a date than were physicians in larger communities.[13] Does this mean that rural practitioners are morally inferior to their urban counterparts?

Doctors practicing in small communities inevitably come in contact with their patients in nonprofessional settings, which may influence how they view the doctor-patient relationship. Wincze et al. found in their survey that therapists in Western Australia were more likely to socialize with their patients than were their American counterparts in Rhode Island: "This finding may be a reflection of cultural differences in which Australian professionals are much more like to go to a hotel [pub] to drink and socialize than their American counterparts."[14] An individual's viewpoint is based on his or her frame of reference. In the case of a doctor who practices in a rural setting, this frame of reference appears to be a factor of the culture as well as isolation from large urban areas.

Physicians in New Zealand participated in several focus groups exploring the issue of sexual misconduct. Regarding urban-rural differences, one conclusion of the focus groups was, "Participants agreed it was impossible to avoid social contact with patients in rural or small town situations where all the residents were potentially patients and friends."[15]

Sex Surrogate Therapy

The hypocrisy of the absolute prohibition of doctor-patient sexual contact is fully appreciated when the discussion of sex surrogate therapy is considered. Although the ethics, efficacy, and need for sex surrogate therapy has been questioned,[16] the open practice of sex surrogates has been reported in the United States, France, Great Britain, and Australia. In the 1960s, Masters and Johnson advocated,sex surrogate partners but later discontinued using such therapy.[17] Rapp reported on an informal study conducted by the College of Physicians and Surgeons of Ontario that discovered the only people apparently in need of sex therapy were young and attractive patients.[18] As previously mentioned, the position of the Canadian Psychiatric Association is unequivocal on the subject of sex used as therapy: "Eroticizing the physician/patient relationship is unacceptable under any circumstances and cannot be rationalized as therapy."[19]

Conversely, a number of articles and authors have discussed the benefits of sex surrogate therapy being useful in the treatment of sexual dysfunction,[20,21] erectile dysfunction,[22] fears of sexuality and intimacy,[23] and heterophobia.[24] Kardener et al. surveyed physicians about when erotic behavior would be indicated as treatment.[25] The respondents indicated that such therapy would be beneficial to help patients recognize their sexual status, for specific sexual problems, to demonstrate there is no physical cause for absence of libido, and to teach sexual anatomy. In 1986, a survey conducted by Herman et al. indicated that 3.9% to 17.9% of responding psychotherapists believed that sexual contact was "always or sometimes appropriate" when treating sexual dysfunction.[26] The range in this finding reflects the breakdown of attitudes among those who admitted to having had sex with patients (17.9%) and those who did not (3.9%).

How does the use of sex surrogate therapy reconcile with the behavioral sciences being the champions of strict standards prohibiting doctor-patient sexual relationships? Other questions further blur the alleged black-and-white issue of concurrent sexual and doctor-patient relationships: Should an emergency room physician be prohibited from dating a patient, in perpetuity, because of a one-time, 15-minute doctor-patient encounter? If a doctor treated another doctor, would there still be a power imbalance to prevent a romantic relationship? If a doctor, through the power and influence of that position, obtained the phone number of a person he or she did not treat, does this constitute unethical behavior?[27] While the treatment of a spouse might be considered unethical, does the dual relationship between spouse and doctor represent sexual misconduct? If protection against allegations of sexual misconduct is allowed for the bond of husband and wife, what status is to be given to homosexual partners?

■ Former Patients

The issue of sexual contact between health-care professionals and their former patients yields even less uniformity of thought than the issue related to current patients. Many of the same organizations and regulatory boards have adopted similar policies against practitioners engaging in sexual and romantic relationships with former patients.[28,29,30] However, there is, once again, no consensus on the subject.[31] In fact, the current language used by many organizations and regulatory agencies in prohibiting relationships with former patients yields regulations which are as vague and possibly unenforceable as those prohibiting sexual relationships with current patients.[32]

Shopland and VandeCreek concluded that there remains an ethical debate about doctors having sexual relations with former patients.[33] They opine, "it would not be entirely incongruent ... to argue that a sexual relationship with an ex-client need not be unethical if the transference has been resolved." This statement brings time into the equation: How long does it take to properly resolve issues of transference?

For psychologists in Florida, the professional relationship is "deemed to continue in perpetuity."[34] Likewise, in Tennessee, some medical doctor–patient relationships "may never terminate because of the nature and extent of the relationship."[35] Colorado and California advocate waiting periods of 6 months and 2 years, respectively, before allowing a psychotherapist to begin a sexual relationship with a former patient. Appelbaum and Jorgenson proposed that time should be the primary factor determining the propriety of sexual relations with former patients.[36] In addition, these authors found no strong evidence to conclude that a therapist–former patient sexual relationship is any more harmful than other consensual, problematic relationships. In response to Appelbaum and Jorgenson's findings, Brown et al. stated, "We do not believe that it is justified, clinically or ethically, for a therapist to engage in sexual intimacy with a patient or former patient, *regardless of the amount of time that has elapsed* between the termination and the sexual intimacy" (emphasis added).[37]

Although the dominant view in the literature of the medical professions and behavioral sciences is that a practitioner should not have a sexual relationship with a former client or patient, there are no clear guidelines. The regulatory boards and professional associations in these fields fail to present a unified position on the subject of ethical standards for sexual relationships between doctors and former patients. Some states take no ethical or regulatory position on sexual relations with former patients, while others advocate a permanent prohibition.[38]

The issue of fraudulent termination of the doctor-patient relationship to advance a romantic or sexual relationship has been discussed in the psychotherapy field. For example, in 1987, the American Psychological Association stated, "If it seems that the treatment ended in order to give the appearance of compliance with the ethical proscription against psychologist-client sexual intimacies . . . such terminations are seen as subterfuge."[39] Therefore, the way in which the doctor-patient relationship ended may be as important as why it was terminated.

■ Current and Former Doctor-Patient Relationships in the Chiropractic Profession

Although the chiropractic literature is silent on the issue of sexual relations between chiropractors and their former patients, some state regulatory boards and professional associations have addressed the issue, evidently using the paradigms of other health-care providers.

As with the medical professions and behavioral sciences, the regulations governing chiropractic practices across the United States reflect a lack of agreement on the issue of sexual relationships with current and former patients. The Federation of Chiropractic Licensing Boards (FCLB) questioned their 50 member boards in the United States regarding sexual boundary issues (unpublished data; see Appendix A). Forty-one of the 50 states (not all states answered each question) responded to the following questions:

1. Does your board have statutes or regulations concerning doctor-patient sexual relations?

   35 states = Yes

   4 states = No

   Comments: The four states that did not have specific statutes in this area stated that such conduct would not be allowed by other aspects of their board regulations prohibiting "moral turpitude, lewd conduct, harassing behavior" or other general language that can be interpreted to accommodate the complaint.

2. Does your board specifically prohibit sexual relations between the doctor and patients who are active or currently under care?

   28 states = Yes

   10 states = No

3. Does your board specifically prohibit sexual relations between the doctor and patients who are inactive or formerly under care? If yes, how long is the doctor specifically prohibited from having sexual relations after care ends?

   13 states = Yes

   26 states = No

Of the states responding "yes," the range of time prohibiting dating former patients ranged from 90 days to 2 years. Some states, however, gave less clear answers to the length of time the doctor would be prohibited from dating a former patient. This includes statements such as "after a reasonable time" and "once the patient understands the doctor/patient relationship has ended."

The answers to the three questions involve physical relationships and the more traditional boundaries concerning sexual relations. The FCLB survey also asked the 50 state boards about regulations covering areas other than physical contact, such as inappropriate verbal communications about sexual activity and improper sexual communications occurring through the mail or over the Internet. Interestingly, many of the boards specifically prohibited these nonphysical categories of sexual boundary violations. Some might believe that regulations concerning nonphysical sexual improprieties would not be necessary, but one board indicated they had filed a disciplinary action against "a licensee who instant messaged a patient and sent nude pictures of himself to the patient over the Internet." The potential for boundary violations with e-mail, chat rooms, instant messaging, downloading images, and placing video or pictures of patients on the Internet would certainly support the creation of specific regulations in this area.[40]

A review of the regulations against sexual misconduct established by various chiropractic regulatory boards across the United States reveals a wide spectrum. Some states—including California, the state with the largest population of chiropractors—have no language concerning sexual relations with a former patient. Some regulatory language requires the chiropractor to simply wait a specified amount of time before sexual relations can ethically occur.[41,42,43] There are even diverging opinions about whether a waiting period should be a fixed amount of time or left to be determined. For example, the Nevada regulatory board allows sexual relations between a chiropractor and a former patient after "a reasonable time."[44] Other states require more than simply the passage of time before sexual relationships with former patients are considered ethical. In addition to imposing a 6-month waiting period between termination of the doctor-patient relationship and the start of a sexual relationship, the Texas regulatory board requires the doctor to ensure that the patient is "no longer emotionally dependent (transference)."[45]

It is important to point out that charges of unprofessional conduct can arise even in states that have no specific regulations about sexual relations between chiropractors and their current or former patients. In these instances, the determination of "unprofessional conduct" is based on an interpretation of other regulations that could apply to a specific situation. For example, Connecticut has no specific regulations in this area but may consider such conduct to be "illegal, negligent or incompetent" and proceed with an action against the doctor. "In such cases, the standard of care is established through testimony, or they may rely on the precedent of past cases."[46] Iowa regulatory language prohibits chiropractors from "engaging in unethical conduct or practice harmful or detrimental to the public."[47] The vagueness of such language allows for many different interpretations of what is considered sexual misconduct.

Because time is the most quoted element when considering sexual relationships with former patients, the issue of exactly when and how a doctor-patient relationship ended must be examined.

■ Terminating the Doctor-Patient Relationship in the Chiropractic Profession

Chiropractic care differs from many other medical specialties in the way the doctor-patient relationship is formally terminated. For example, if a woman undergoes a successful hysterectomy, she might never see the surgeon again; the doctor-patient relationship ends after the specific condition is treated. By contrast, with many chiropractic professionals emphasizing lifelong spinal hygiene, some chiropractor-patient relationships may never formally end.

It would be unwise for a chiropractor to conclude that a doctor-patient relationship had been terminated simply because the patient had not come in for a year. If termination of the relationship is desired and/or necessary, it is advisable to end care with a formalized and definitive step rather than merely with the simple passage of time. Given the scope of laws and the varying sociopolitical differences on this subject, legal counsel should be consulted when the need for formal termination of the doctor-patient relationship arises. The steps leading to formally ending a doctor-patient relationship vary depending on the reason for the termination. If the doctor perceived the potential for unethical transference or countertransference issues in the relationship but no sexual contact had occurred, legal counsel might recommend the following steps for terminating the doctor-patient relationship:

- Document the patient's chart.
- Formally notify the patient that the doctor-patient relationship is to be terminated.
- If continued care is indicated, recommend several other qualified chiropractors in the area.

These steps may be adequate for the normal cessation of the doctor-patient relationship. What if the care is ending because a sexual relationship is desired between consenting adults? The doctor is now entering an area of higher risk because such conduct does not meet with universal acceptance. Consultation with legal counsel is therefore strongly recommended. Trying to maneuver through the land mines of ethical, moral, and legal requirements when considering a post-termination sexual relationship without legal counsel is akin to driving blindfolded down the freeway. Improperly ending the doctor-patient relationship to advance a personal relationship could lead to allegations of false termination.[48]

Ambiguity about when the doctor-patient relationship actually ended may be the basis for disciplinary action. The literature reveals no relevant cases involving the chiropractic profession, but a case filed by the nursing board of Utah illustrates the possible actions against any health-care provider. A 1991 Utah Court of Appeals decision addressed this issue in a case in which the nursing board disciplined a male nurse who entered a sexual relationship with a female patient after her release from a psychiatric facility where the nurse was employed. After the patient was discharged, the nurse shared an apartment with the patient and her husband and continued to assist in caring for the patient, without payment for services. The nurse claimed that he was helping the patient "as a friend." The court ruled that the relationship had not been terminated clearly and definitely and allowed the nursing board to take disciplinary action.[49]

■ Nonsexual Relationships Between Chiropractors and Current and Former Patients

Nonsexual relationships with patients, such as social friendships and business partnerships, can also pose ethical difficulties for the doctor of chiropractic.[50] These so-called dual relationships are addressed in the ACA's code of ethics, which states the following:[51]

> The physician/patient relationship *requires* the doctor of chiropractic to exercise utmost care that he or she will do nothing to "exploit the trust and dependency of the patient." Doctors of chiropractic should make every effort to *avoid dual relationships* that could impair their professional judgment or risk the possibility of exploiting the confidence placed in them by the patient (emphasis added).

Pipes discussed potential ethical problems for psychologists forming nonsexual personal relationships with former clients.[52] The author makes a strong argument against forming nonsexual relationships with former patients for the following reasons. Although the practice of chiropractic and psychotherapy differ, Pipes' observations are relevant and worth consideration.

1. The former patient may need to return to care. A significant business relationship initiated after care ends would make return to treatment difficult because a business relationship can skew the practitioner's clinical objectivity or alter the patient's levels of trust and respect for the practitioner's treatment opinions.
2. Some patients are mentally or emotionally vulnerable and may improperly rely on the practitioner in other types of relationships. Such vulnerability may leave patients open to being taken advantage of and result in their financial harm.
3. The practitioner may be required to furnish records or testify in court concerning the details of past care. Examples of this would be professional opinions in court about injuries, pain, suffering, and future care. In such cases, the practitioner must be an independent observer of the patient's clinical condition and remain unbiased by a personal or business connection.
4. It is reasonable to attempt to manage the professional risk of practice. Some risks can be minimized, and avoiding sexual and nonsexual relationships with former patients would help reduce the possible risk of legal complications and state board actions.

In summary, it is currently considered unprofessional, and sometimes illegal, to engage in sexual relations with a current patient. The consideration to enter into a sexual relationship with a former patient must not be considered lightly, no matter where one practices. If the doctor wishes to develop such a relationship, it should be done with great care to comply with applicable laws and regulations. The doctor must be forewarned that consulting legal counsel and following the letter of regulatory law is not always enough to avoid civil actions. Such actions typically cite transference and countertransference issues as contaminating and/or voiding the formalized termination of the doctor-patient relationship.

Endnotes

1. American Medical Association, Council on Ethical and Judicial Affairs. Sexual misconduct in the practice of medicine. JAMA 1991;266:2741–2745.
2. Sexual behaviour and physicians [policy statement]. Ottawa: Society of Obstetricians and Gynaecologists of Canada, 1992.
3. American Psychiatric Association. The Principles of Medical Ethics with Annotations Especially Applicable to Psychiatry. Rev ed. Washington, DC: American Psychiatric Association, 1995: section 2, annotation 1.
4. Canadian Medical Association policy statement. CMAJ 1994;150.
5. Sreenivasan U. Sexual exploitation of patients: the position of the Canadian Psychiatric Association. Can J Psychiatry 1989;34:234–237.
6. Royal Australian and New Zealand College of Psychiatrists Code of Ethics. Melbourne, Victoria: Royal Australian and New Zealand College of Psychiatrists, 1990.
7. Fla Stat Ann 466.027 (1992).
8. Sexual misconduct statement of the West Virginia Board of Medicine. W V Med J 1993;89:276–277.
9. Coleman PG. Sexual relationships between therapist and patient—different countries, different treatment. J Psychiatry Law 1988;16:577–623.
10. Coleman PG. Sexual relationships between therapist and patient—different countries, different treatment. Jour. Psychiatry & Law; winter 1988;577–623.
11. Jorgenson L, Randles R, Strasburger L. The furor over psychotherapist-patient sexual contact: new solutions to old problems. William and Mary Law Review 1991;32:645–732.
12. Simon RI. Therapist-patient sex: from boundary violations to sexual misconduct. Psychiatr Clin North Am 1999;22:31–47.
13. Sheps SB, Schechter M. Attitudes and behaviours in physician-patient relationships: results of surveys of physicians and the public in British Columbia. Vancouver: University of British Columbia, 1993.
14. Wincze JP, Richards J, Parsons J, Bailey S. A comparative survey of therapist sexual misconduct between an American state and an Australian state. Prof Psychol Res Pr 1996;27:289–294.
15. White GE, Coverdale JA, Thomson AN. Can one be a good doctor and have a sexual relationship with one's patient? Fam Pract 1994;11:389–393.
16. Hopwood C. Surrogate therapy for sexual dysfunction [letter to editor]. Med J Aust 1992;156:143.
17. Richardson JD. Has surrogate therapy a place in treating sexual dysfunction? Med J Aust 1991;155:689–690.
18. Rapp MS. Sexual misconduct. CMAJ 1997;137:193–194.
19. Sreenivasan U. Sexual exploitation of patients: the position of the Canadian Psychiatric Association. Can J Psychiatry 1989;34:234–237.
20. Richardson JD. Has surrogate therapy a place in treating sexual dysfunction? Med J Aust 1991;155:689–690.
21. Cole M. Surrogate's role in sexual inadequacy. Br J Sex Med 1976;3:35–36.
22. Reynolds B. Psychological treatment of erectile dysfunction in men without partners: outcome results and a new direction. J Sex Marital Ther 1991;17:136–146.
23. Kluft RP. The physician as perpetrator of abuse. Prim Care 1993;20:459–480.
24. Brewer C. Cure of heterophobia by sexual surrogate therapy. Br Med J 1981;1055.
25. Kardener SH, Fuller M, Mensh I. A survey of physicians' attitudes and practices regarding erotic and non-erotic contact with patients. Am J Psychiatry 1973;130:1077–1081.

26. Herman JL, Gartrell N, Olarte S, Feldstein M, Localio R. Psychiatrist-patient sexual contact: results of a national survey, II: psychiatrists' attitudes. Am J Psychiatry 1987;144:164–169.

27. Shaw D. Sexual involvement between physicians and patients: regulations are not a panacea. CMAJ 1994;150:1397–1399.

28. American Medical Association, Council on Ethical and Judicial Affairs. Sexual misconduct in the practice of medicine. JAMA 1991;266:2741–2745.

29. Sexual behaviour and physicians [policy statement]. Ottawa: Society of Obstetricians and Gynaecologists of Canada, 1992.

30. Jones LE, Adkins E. Allegations of sexual misconduct: a risk management perspective. J Healthc Risk Manag 1997;17:8–14.

31. Appelbaum PS, Jorgenson LM, Sutherland PK. Sexual relationships between physicians and patients. Arch Intern Med 1994;154:2561–2565.

32. Coleman PG. Sexual relationships between therapist and patient—different countries, different treatment. J Psychiatry Law 1988;16:577–623.

33. Shopland SN, VandeCreek L. Sex with ex-clients: theoretical rationales for prohibition. Ethics Behav 1991;1:35–44.

34. Florida, Department of Health, Board of Psychology, Rule 64B19–16.003 Chapter 21U-15.004.

35. Tennessee State Board of Medical Examiners. Sexual misconduct statement and policy. J Tenn Med Assoc 1994;87:19–20.

36. Appelbaum PS, Jorgenson L. Psychotherapist-patient sexual contact after termination: an analysis and a proposal. Am J Psychiatry 1991;148:1466–1473.

37. Brown LS, Borys DS, Brodsky AM, et al. Psychotherapist-patient sexual contact after termination of treatment [author reply 987-9]. Am J Psychiatry 1992;149:979–980.

38. Gutheil TG. How to Avoid Mental Health Malpractice: Useful Clinical Strategies. Preston, CA.: Medicine and Behavior/Continuing Medical Education, 1988.

39. American Psychological Association Monitor, June 1987, pg. 45.

40. Walsh D. Seven-year sentence in child porn case. The judge blasts a Yuba City chiropractor who filmed patients. Sacramento Bee, November 20, 2001.

41. Maine Board of Chiropractic Licensure, 233 CMR 4.06(n-o).

42. Mississippi Board of Chiropractic Examiners, Rules and Regulations, Code of Ethics, §11.14.

43. Ga Reg 100-7-.01(f)(1).

44. Nev Adm Code 634.430,3(d)(2).

45. Rules and Regulations of the Texas Board of Chiropractic Examiners, §75.1(c).

46. Conn Gen Stat 19a-14(F).

47. Iowa Board of Chiropractic Examiners, Rules and Regulations, §645-45.1(3).

48. Pipes RB. Nonsexual relationships between psychotherapists and their former clients: obligations of psychologists. Ethics Behav 1997;7:27–41.

49. Heinecke v Department of Commerce, 810 P2d 459 (Utah Ct App 1991).

50. White GE, Coverdale JA, Thomson AN. Can one be a good doctor and have a sexual relationship with one's patient? Fam Pract 1994;11:389–393.

51. American Chiropractic Association, Code of Ethics, A(6), A(7), A(10), C(2).

52. Pipes RB. Nonsexual relationships between psychotherapists and their former clients: obligations of psychologists. Ethics Behav 1997;7:27–41.

Legal Implications of Sexual Misconduct

11

As previous chapters have shown, the range of behaviors that various national, state, and organizational agencies consider sexual misconduct includes telling a joke, hugging, having a "romantic relationship" with a former patient, and engaging in sexual intercourse with a current patient. In the present zero-tolerance environment, and under the ambiguous language of current regulations, all may result in allegations and possible legal action. The American legal system has several venues in which to hear such allegations, each with a different legal mandate. In fact, a health-care professional accused of alleged sexual misconduct could face many different legal actions imposed by many different legal entities, each with a unique set of rules and evidence standards.

Any allegation of sexual misconduct can initiate an ever-cascading continuum of legal trouble. Once the legal Pandora's box has been opened, a plethora of other legal events is likely to follow. Even if the doctor manages to defeat every allegation, most certainly the doctor will never be able to overcome the tremendous financial and personal losses that will undoubtedly occur over years of protracted legal proceedings.

■ Civil Legal System

The civil legal system allows for a venue where injured parties can seek recompense for damages they alleged to have incurred. This court system has the lowest standard of evidence for a determination of finding. The plaintiff must convince the jury by a "preponderance of the evidence," which in practical terms equates to a mere tipping of the evidence in favor of the plaintiff.

It is in the civil court system that a patient can bring a claim of malpractice against a health-care provider of any specialty. If the plaintiff proves negligence and damages for breaching of standards of care, the jury is then asked to award an appropriate amount of money to attempt to make the plaintiff whole. In 1995, Simon reported that among insurance companies providing malpractice coverage to psychiatrists, 20% of their costs were for cases of sexual misconduct.[1] For psychologists and psychiatrists, sexual involvement with a patient is one of the most common causes of malpractice litigation.[2] Consequently, some companies place strict limits on coverage in this area.[3] Moreover, defending and indemnifying acts of sexual misconduct typically are not responsibilities that malpractice insurers accept.[4] Even if a malpractice carrier provides a doctor with a defense when an act of sexual malpractice is alleged, the carrier will generally refuse to pay any damages related to the sexual misconduct and may also attempt to recover the cost of the defense.[5] The cost of all legal representation, outside possible claims of negligence, are borne solely by the doctor.

Because of the sensitive and emotional nature of sexual misconduct cases, other types of civil legal actions often arise. The manner of these other civil proceedings is inevitably proportional to the seriousness of the allegations. For example, a doctor accused of having sexual relations with minors in his office might subsequently face divorce proceedings and child custody battles. In some states, the spouse of a patient who has been sexually involved with a doctor can file a separate civil suit against the doctor for loss of consortium (the legal term for loss of intimate relations with a spouse).[6]

A sexual misconduct case might also include allegations of battery—defined as "an unprivileged, intentional and harmful or offensive contact between one person and another"[7]—as well as allegations of "intentional and negligent infliction of emotional distress"—which usually arise in sexual misconduct cases that involve consensual sex and can be difficult to refute. A review of the literature on sexual misconduct cases reveals that priests have had civil allegations successfully filed for intentional and negligent infliction of emotional distress. For example, a Colorado case involved a female parishioner who went to her priest for marriage counseling and eventually had a sexual relationship with the priest. The court rejected her claim of clergy malpractice but did uphold her claim of intentional and negligent infliction of emotional distress. The court also found the priest's conduct to be "outrageous in character and so extreme in degree as to go beyond all possible bounds of decency."[8]

A doctor facing serious allegations of professional boundary violations could also face a breach-of-contract suit filed by business partners attempting to recoup losses resulting from the sexual misconduct charges. If one of a group of doctors is charged with, say, possession of child pornography, the entire group can be adversely affected.

Civil remedies to address fraud may also arise from allegations of sexual misconduct. A doctor committing professional boundary violations during the course of treating a patient is billing an insurance carrier and receiving reimbursement for that treatment. However, is the doctor receiving money for care that was reasonable and/or necessary? Is the doctor being unjustly rewarded for a nonclinical agenda? If the doctor received reimbursement for care that was not reasonable, those who paid for said care could sue the doctor for fraud.

■ State Regulatory Boards

Regulatory boards, aka administrative boards, are publicly funded agencies entrusted with protecting the public by ensuring a minimal level of competency for licensing the professionals who provide services to the public. The rules governing the various vocations and professions are typically codified in state regulations and acts. If there is an allegation of a breach of conduct, the regulatory board conducts an administrative court proceeding, which is overseen by a judge or hearing officer, but typically no jury is involved. The standards necessary for determining guilt in an administrative hearing typically require "clear and convincing evidence." This legal burden is greater than that needed in civil courts but less than that required in criminal trials. The actions an administrative court can take in breach-of-conduct cases are limited to revoking or suspending the professional's license, imposing a fine, or issuing a citation.

Because the mandate of the administrative system is different than that of civil courts, a doctor accused of sexual transgressions may face actions in both administrative court and civil court at the same time. Malpractice insurance coverage does not extend to actions brought by regulatory boards. Therefore, a doctor facing charges in administrative court must bear all costs for legal representation.[9]

It is important to realize that each state has its own administrative system and its own regulatory language concerning relationships between doctors and their patients. Even in states that lack specific language concerning sexual misconduct, other sections of regulatory language may have general prohibitions for unprofessional conduct.

■ Criminal Justice System

Like the administrative system, the criminal justice system has the mandate to protect the public. However, the protection provided by the criminal justice system extends well beyond licensing and can include incarcerating professionals accused of sexual misconduct. The severity of the sanction inspired a more stringent burden of proof in criminal cases: Convictions require a finding of guilt "beyond a reasonable doubt." A criminal conviction represents the highest level of evidence of any court proceeding. All legal representation and associated costs needed to defend a doctor from criminal allegations are once again borne solely by the doctor.

Until the early 1960s, the criminal justice system only became involved in cases alleging sexual misconduct by a health-care professional in two instances: when the patient was underage or when the sexual advances were unwanted by the patient. In 1976, Masters and Johnson suggested that a therapist who becomes sexually involved with a patient should be charged with rape rather than malpractice, whether or not the sexual relationship was consensual.[10]

In 1994, Congress recognized the seriousness of unwanted sexual touching by passing the Violence Against Women Act. The act declared "unwanted sexual touching a crime of violence." The provisions of the act were tested in a 1997 case against a Provo, Utah, chiropractor. Three former employees of the chiropractor filed a federal lawsuit for damages, claiming the doctor "repeatedly fondled and rubbed their buttocks, breasts, and genital areas without their consent."[11] The doctor denied the allegations, and a federal trial judge ruled that the women could not invoke the provision of the Violence Against Women Act because they had not alleged any violence during the time the unwanted sexual touching allegedly occurred.

The three employees filed an appeal, and the 10th U.S. Circuit Court of Appeals overturned the earlier court decision. The appeals court opined that they would not limit "the definition of violence to only those forms of violence most traditionally feared by men—murder and serious bodily injury." The doctor then filed an appeal, claiming that many states do not include nonconsensual sexual touching in their definitions of violent sex offenses. In a 5 to 4 decision, the Supreme Court set aside the prior ruling. The Court ruled that Congress had overstepped its authority by including unwanted sexual touching as a "gender-motivated crime of violence" in the Violence Against Women Act and held that the determination of violence with unwanted sexual touching is an issue for each state. The federal appeals court was therefore instructed to reconsider the Utah dispute, and the three women were forced to sue the doctor for civil damages under Utah state law as opposed to federal law.[12]

Health-care professionals accused of criminal acts against adult patients are likely to face some jail time, but incarceration is almost a certainty in cases involving underage patients.

Criminal charges are not limited to physical contact between a doctor and a patient. With the advent of technology, new areas of misconduct are evolving. An example of this is the complaint filed in 2001 by the attorney general against a chiropractor with the "production of a visual depiction of a minor engaging in sexually explicit conduct."[13] The unsuspecting victims, both minors and adults, were instructed to disrobe completely and then change into hospital gowns. The patients were then told to perform various flexibility exercises while standing directly over a hidden camera, which was concealed in the floor of the X-ray room. Investigators confiscated 380 videotapes in the chiropractor's office when they served their search warrant. The doctor stated that he intended to place the videos on the Internet to fund his retirement.[14] The doctor surrendered his license to practice to the state board and sent to prison.[15] In another case, a California chiropractor was indicted in November 2002 for possession of child pornography.[16] The mere possession of such material is considered a federal offense, whether it is located in a home or an office. The doctor was alleged to be part of an international ring selling pornographic images worldwide. Investigators in California reviewed more than *one million images* stored on the chiropractor's computer on 400 confiscated compact discs. The doctor surrendered his license to the regulatory board after an accusation was filed.[17]

Criminal sanctions against doctors having sexual relations with patients became more common through the 1990s. Advocates argued that criminal penalties were needed for four reasons: (1) The activity is repugnant, (2) penalties would deter the same behavior in others, (3) penalties are the best method to incapacitate the offender and protect others, and (4) penalties can be a form of treatment for the offender.[18]

Jorgenson et al. reported that sexual contact between a therapist and a patient is a criminal offense in 13 states: California, Connecticut, Colorado, Florida, Georgia, Iowa, Maine, Minnesota, New Mexico, North Dakota, South Dakota, Texas, and Wisconsin.[19] No chiropractor should derive comfort from the fact that many state statutes are specifically written for psychologists and psychiatrists. Medical physicians have found that they may be held to this standard. Searight and Campbell stated, "From a strictly legal perspective, physicians should be aware that they may soon be held to a standard similar to that for their colleagues in psychiatry."[20] Chiropractors should take this warning seriously because the wording of some statutes is fairly broad and may be interpreted to include chiropractors under either the term *physician* or *unlicensed practitioner*. Borruso stated, "The term 'unlicensed practitioner' refers to the increasing number of therapists who practice one or more alternative therapies that traditional practitioners often do not recognize (for example, holistic medicine and new age therapy).[21] Minnesota's law against therapist-patient sex contains a detailed list of those who may be included under the term *psychotherapists*.[22] The list includes "physicians, psychologists, nurses, chemical dependency counselors, social workers, clergy, marriage and family therapists, mental health service providers and others who purport to perform psychotherapy."[23] Wisconsin's law against sexual misconduct by therapists contains a nearly identical list of people that may also be considered psychotherapists.[24]

Chiropractors who limit their practice to a traditional form of spinal adjustment may find it hard to understand their profession could be categorized as psychotherapy. However, many chiropractors use techniques that combine spinal adjustments and "emotional" therapies, such as the Neuro Emotional Technique (NET). The NET Web site describing topics at an advanced NET seminar states, "You are taught new variations of NET, such as developing verbal suppositions and personal laws, which have influenced your patient/client's 'Neuro Emotional Complexes.' You will also learn more on the art of rapport, transference, counter-transference, etc."[25] Such nontraditional chiropractic care could be construed as psychotherapeutic and prompt states to regulate the chiropractic profession as they do the behavioral science professions.

The movement to criminalize sexual relations between psychotherapists and patients continues to grow, and a call for a federal criminal statute has been made.[26] The proponents of this movement argue that criminal penalties are required because sanctions against a therapist's license under the administrative system are not sufficiently serious to deter sexual misconduct.

■ State Associations and Professional Societies

Depending on the outcome of criminal and/or administrative hearings, a state association may ask for a doctor's membership to be withdrawn. Because there are no required rules of evidence for such proceedings, such disciplinary actions are often quite arbitrary and political in nature. The doctor may choose to fight such proceedings to protect any managed care contracts from being voided. Once again, the doctor pays all legal costs for such proceedings. Malpractice and other business insurance policies do not cover attorneys' fees arising from the actions of professional associations or societies.

Endnotes

1. Simon RI. Sexual Misconduct of therapists: a cause for civil and criminal action. Trial 1995;21:46–51.
2. Pope KS. Research and laws regarding therapist-patient sexual involvement: implications for therapists. Am J Psychother 1986;40:564–571.
3. Appelbaum PS. Statutes regulating patient-therapist sex. Hosp Community Psychiatry 1990;41:15–16.
4. Crane M. Protect yourself against a sexual-misconduct charge. Med Econ 1996;73:90, 92, 98 passim.
5. Stahl MJ, Foreman SM. Sexual Misconduct: Ethical, Clinical and Legal Ramifications and the Chiropractic Profession. Des Moines, IA: NCMIC, 1997.
6. Simon RI. Clinical Psychiatry and the Law. 2nd ed. Washington, DC: American Psychiatric Press, 1992.
7. Keeton WP, ed. Prosser and Keeton on the Law of Torts. 5th ed. St. Paul, MN: West, 1984.
8. Destefano v. Grabian, 763 P.2d 275 (Colo. 1988).
9. Crane M. Protect yourself against a sexual-misconduct charge. Med Econ 1996;73:90, 92, 98 passim.
10. Masters WH, Johnson VE. Principles of the new sex therapy. Am J Psychiatry 1976;133:548–554.

11. Carelli R. Court bumps Provo case. Daily Herald, May 23, 2000.

12. McCann v Rosquist, 185 F3d 1113, 1119-20 (10th Cir. 1999).

13. Gormley L. FBI files video peeping charge. Appeal-Democrat, January 5, 2001.

14. Walsh D. Seven-year sentence in child porn case. Sacramento Bee, November 20, 2001.

15. California Board of Chiropractic Examiners, Default Decision No. 2001-228, May 2001.

16. Soto O. 15 indicted in global child-pornography ring. Union-Tribune, August 10, 2002.

17. California Board of Chiropractic Examiners, Accusation No. 2003-325, December 23, 2002.

18. Hoge SK, Jorgenson L, Goldstein N, Metzner J, Patterson R, Robinson G. APA resource document: legal sanctions for mental health professional-patient sexual misconduct. Bull Am Acad Psychiatry Law 1995;23:433–448.

19. Jorgenson L, Randles R, Strasburger L. The furor over psychotherapist-patient sexual contact. William and Mary Law Review 1991;32:645–732.

20. Searight HR, Campbell DC. Physician-patient sexual contact: ethical and legal issues and clinical guidelines. J Fam Pract 1993;36:647–653.

21. Borruso MT. Sexual abuse by psychotherapists: the call for a uniform criminal statue. Am J Law Med 1991;17:289–311.

22. Minn Stat Ann §609.345 (1990).

23. Minn Stat Ann §609.341 (17) (West 1987).

24. Wis Stat §940.22 (1986).

25. NET seminars page. NET Inc. Web site. Available at: http://www.netmindbody.com/seminars.html#mind.

26. Borruso MT. Sexual abuse by psychotherapists: the call for a uniform criminal statue. Am J Law Med 1991;17:289–311.

Preventing False Allegations and Boundary Violations

The practice of chiropractic goes hand in hand with a certain amount of legal risk. As was pointed out in the proceeding chapter, this legal risk can come in a variety of forms, including malpractice suits, allegations of criminal malfeasance, and actions by regulatory board. No matter how hard a doctor might try, there is no way to eliminate all risk associated with the practice of chiropractic, other than to leave the profession. Consequently, the only option is to develop rules and procedures that will help manage the profession's inherent risk. Successful risk management allows the doctor the freedom to practice with reason and efficiency.

In our experience speaking to chiropractors on risk management, we have found that the concept is difficult for many to understand and often becomes clearer when we use the analogy of driving an automobile. Insurance actuaries and their companies base policy rates on their ability to identify the risks of driving. These companies use past driving performance and other risky behaviors as determining factors for the cost of premiums. For example, receiving three speeding tickets in one year would be associated with risky behavior. Young male drivers have been proven to use less skill and drive faster, two behaviors that increase their chances of being in an accident. Thus, insurance rates for young males are higher than those for females of similar age and with similar driving records.

Prudent drivers wanting to manage their risk would obey all traffic laws, stopping at yellow lights instead of accelerating through the intersection, and wearing seat belts. However, no amount of risk management by one driver can eliminate the possibility of getting into an accident because someone else drove the wrong way on the highway, blindfolded, drunk, and without a seat belt—an obvious example of poor risk management.

Much the same can be said for the management of risk in a chiropractic office. Chiropractors participate in situations that might be misunderstood by the patient or that might put their professional standing at the apex of a legally slippery slope.

The preventive measures presented in the following sections are for concerned practitioners who recognize the monumental professional, social, and financial risks from allegations of sexual boundary violations and want to properly manage that risk. The suggestions are not intended to serve as a "bulletproof vest" for any doctor guilty of sexual misconduct.

■ Verbal Communications

All verbal communications in the professional setting should be geared toward professional interaction with and treatment of patients. Although exchanging certain pleasantries as part of a typical office encounter is expected, inappropriate language, such as telling sexual jokes, serves only to damage the respect between doctor and patient that is so hard to regain. Inappropriate comments are not limited to off-color jokes but include any remark that could embarrass a patient or be construed as being erotic in nature.

■ Physical Interactions

Although by its very nature the practice of chiropractic involves a great deal of physical interaction between doctor and patient, many people outside the profession do not understand the necessity of hands-on care. The practice of chiropractic involves two forms of physical contact: examinations and treatment.

■ Examinations

A chiropractor's physical interaction with a patient begins on the first day the patient enters the office. The initial visit typically includes an examination that requires physical contact between the chiropractor and the patient. The doctor usually checks the patient's heart, lungs, and abdomen and does palpation of peripheral pulses as well as palpation to detect spinal subluxations. The hands-on nature of chiropractic spinal analysis may require the patient to be gowned. Because chiropractors place their hands on patients during initial and subsequent office visits, at times when the patient is gowned, some people consider the examination process a potentially risky behavior. The following preventive measures could help avoid misunderstandings and properly manage such risk.

Initial Examinations

All initial examinations should be performed during normal business hours. This is especially important when the patient is of the opposite sex. An examination conducted after hours, when the chiropractor is the only staff member in the office, is an opportunity for misunderstandings and allegations of improper conduct and thus an example of poor risk management.

The doctor should consider performing initial examinations in a room close to the front office so another staff member could be called easily to be a chaperone during a portion of the examination if necessary. An examination room located in the back of the office can be seen as purposely designed to prevent anyone from hearing any claims of misconduct.

Chaperoning Practices

It is not standard practice in the chiropractic profession to use a chaperone during a patient examination, nor are we advocating this be done on a routine basis. However, at times, using a chaperone can help manage the risk of a patient misunderstanding the intent of an examination procedure. If the clinical investigation of the patient requires examination of the patient's genitals, breasts, and/or rectum, a chaperone is recommended. Some practitioners recommend that the patient be given the option to have a third party present during any office visit.

The doctor may also wish to add a question to the patient intake form that asks, "Do you wish to have a third person or chaperone present during your examination and treatment?" Besides identifying patients who are sensitive to personal boundary issues before they even enter the examination room, this question also alerts the staff of the need for a chaperone and relieves the patient of the embarrassment of having to ask for the presence of a third party.

Another situation in which the chiropractor should strongly consider using a chaperone is when a patient is making inappropriate comments or actions and the doctor believes that these may escalate into overt problems. The presence of a third party in the room will usually stop inappropriate behavior. In addition, a third party should be present when the chiropractor terminates a doctor-patient relationship. Finally, a doctor who recognizes signs of countertransference developing toward a patient should consider using a chaperone. The third person will discourage inappropriate behavior from the doctor to the patient as well.

Gowning and Draping

Examination gowns are to be used when necessary. Gowns that afford the greatest degree of privacy but still allow for competent clinical examination of the area in question should be used.

Explicit instructions regarding the articles of clothing that need to be removed should be given to the patient; for example, "Please remove your shoes, socks, pants and shirt, but do not remove any of your undergarments. Wear the gown with the opening in the back. Be sure to close the gown using the Velcro or ties on the back." The patient should be asked to slightly open the examination room door to acknowledge that he or she has finished gowning. This prevents the awkward situation where the doctor walks in while the patient is still in the process of gowning. By having the patient open the door, the patient is initiating the examination process.

When the clinical investigation includes placing the patient in a prone position, draping a towel over the buttocks is suggested. Again, this affords the patient every possible level of privacy without interfering with the clinical examination.

Testing

The doctor should explain all testing procedures before they occur and obtain the patient's permission to perform any diagnostic test. The

explanation should include the clinical necessity of the test and is especially important when any sexual or private area will be including in the
procedure. For example, the doctor should explain to a female patient
why it is necessary for her to remove her brassiere to have X-rays taken.

Undergarments

Proper chiropractic care would require the patient, male or female,
to remove undergarments around the genital area only in extremely
rare clinical situations. If the removal of undergarments is clinically
required, the doctor is well advised to explain the procedure to the patient. The doctor should consider the use of a chaperone, follow proper
draping procedures, and keep the exposed area as small as possible.

Staff Instructions

Staff should be made keenly aware of gowning, chaperoning, and other
preventive measures used in the practice. This can occur when a staff
member is hired and/or during regular staff meetings.

■ Treatment Procedures

The same risk management measures taken during the initial examination should extend into treatment. When care necessitates access to
the skin, proper gowning instructions and draping procedures are again
recommended. In addition to the recommendations made for the initial examination, the following can assist in proper risk management
when chiropractic treatment is indicated.

Explaining the types of treatments being performed can avoid misunderstanding. Someone with radicular lower extremity secondary to
a piriformis syndrome might not understand the clinical relevance of
ultrasounding the sciatic nerve in the buttock region and therefore the
need to expose the area. Without a proper explanation, the procedure
might be misconstrued as some type of erotic act.

Informed consent is suggested when the doctor anticipates applying a chiropractic technique that is either different from the patient's
prior chiropractic experiences or will require placement of the doctor's
hands in the areas of the genitals or breasts. An example of this would

be a patient who has been treated with high-velocity chiropractic manipulative therapy in the past and then, after clinical determination, was found to need an internal coccyx adjustment.

When treating a minor, even after obtaining the parent's "consent to treat a minor" authorization, parental supervision and/or a chaperone is highly suggested.

■ Written or Printed Materials

All written and printed material in the office setting should be professional and appropriate. It is inappropriate for sexually explicit magazines, cartoons, drawings, or other publications to be found anywhere in the office, including the waiting room, employees' break room, or doctor's office.

The prohibition against unacceptable material also includes office computers, especially those with Internet connections. Office policy should prohibit staff from downloading sexually explicit pictures or written material, and the doctor should take appropriate action immediately on learning about the situation. Keeping such material stored in an office computer is an example of very risky behavior. The doctor may wish to use Internet filters to prevent the staff from downloading and accessing inappropriate Web sites or software programs and to monitor what Internet sites staff members have accessed.

■ Personal Behavior

Summer and McCrory discussed measures that doctors can take to ensure that their personal conduct does not include actions that might enhance or directly lead to both transference and countertransference:[1]

- Do not seek emotional support from patients. It is inappropriate to discuss personal issues, such as personal finances, marital problems, and social or sexual fantasies.
- Do not ask patients to perform personal services for you. Avoid all personal interaction that creates the impression of breaching the doctor-patient relationship. Avoid seeing patients after hours at the office or giving them rides.

- Consider never performing an examination on a patient of the opposite sex without a chaperone. While this is not the standard in the chiropractic profession, it is a step that a chiropractor can take to obtain maximum risk management.
- Recognize your own vulnerability. Be aware of the profile characteristics of patients who may be predisposed to sexual misconduct.
- Be wary of exchanging gifts with patients. This warning includes being lax about fees or allowing fees to mount. Anyone responsible for assessing a sexual boundary allegation may question what types of considerations were in place if no fees were collected.
- If a patient is aggressively seductive, in a calm voice simply say, "This behavior is inappropriate and is not in the best interest of our professional relationship." If termination of the doctor-patient relationship does not occur after this incident, use a chaperone during all subsequent office visits. Pope and Bouhoutsos reported that in 70% of the cases of sexual misconduct, the patient initiated the relationship.[2] Therefore, it is not unreasonable to conclude that, over the course of a career, a doctor will be seduced by a patient at least once.

In its statement on sexual misconduct, the West Virginia Board of Medicine recommended the following practices for doctors faced with at-risk situations:[3]

- Refer the patient to a colleague.
- Seek help for possible countertransference issues or when the patient develops transference issues.
- Increase documentation of all office visits and events. In addition, keep all letters, phone messages, and other written communications.
- Seek legal advice.
- Be aware that treatment boundaries tend to erode gradually over time.

■ Summary of Risk Management

Every health-care provider has ample reason for concern about the consequences of even an allegation of a sexual boundary violation, not to mention being found culpable of such conduct. A doctor can properly manage a certain amount of risk associated with ethical chiropractic practices by having procedures in place and, more importantly, by using common sense. It is advisable to try to view all conduct through the eyes of the uninformed public. Sometimes a doctor's most valuable barometer of office conduct is her or his own family. If the doctor judges a joke, a cartoon, or a comment as acceptable for his or her own children, typically it would be acceptable in the office; otherwise, the material should not be included in the clinical setting. While this seems somewhat straitlaced given what currently appears on television, until the pendulum moves off its hypersensitive arc, the prudent doctor would accept these standards.

From a professional viewpoint, the first step in prevention of sexual boundary transgressions is for the profession to develop standards and to provide education for doctors of chiropractic. At this time, the profession has established no clear standards. Some professional associations have developed their own rules regarding sexual misconduct that conflict with many regulatory board statutes. With the publication of this book, we hope to bring clarity to the issue and prompt the development of uniform standards that are as unique as the chiropractic profession.

Although education regarding sexual misconduct and boundary violations appears to be the knee-jerk panacea for the problem, education may be both helpful and harmful. Education allows the reasonable and ethical doctor of chiropractic to avoid allegations that are borne out of simple cultural or social ignorance on the subject. Unfortunately, some practitioners use the educational process to further their own sexual misconduct. Because chiropractic involves the "laying on of hands," some practitioners use the knowledge obtained from education as an opportunity to find loopholes to explain their unethical behavior. This type of doctor represents the most unethical practitioner, as the doctor is not only committing a sexual offense but also bastardizing the chiropractic profession. Therefore, education only benefits those doctors who desire to practice in a manner that is clear of misconduct.

■ False Allegations of Sexual Misconduct

The harm to a patient who has been exploited by a health-care provider is certainly a serious concern for the public. The profession needs to vehemently decry the conduct of any doctor who truly commits boundary violations. However, before a doctor is condemned by the profession and possibly disciplined by a regulatory agency, the allegations must be determined to have merit. Every allegation of sexual misconduct should be considered true only when enough facts have been gathered to support it. Given the grave consequences for even an allegation of sexual impropriety being made, these safeguards are not unwarranted.

False allegations of professional boundary violations have been reported in the literature, once again, primarily within the behavioral sciences.[4,5] False allegations were also reported to have occurred in a hospital intensive care unit when a 57-year-old male misperceived a rectal intubation as a sexual assault.[6] The same report included a 31-year-old female patient who misinterpreted a perineal bed bath as an erotic act. Chiropractic care can yield similar misinterpretations.[7] For example, in another case of poor communication, a new immigrant to the United States brought allegations of sexual misconduct against a chiropractor. After the chiropractor's actions were explained in a context the patient could understand, the allegations were dropped.

Gutheil indicated, again strictly in regards to the psychotherapy fields, that false allegations are dominated by accusers with borderline personalities.[8] This may be especially important when dealing with allegations where there is no objective or corroborating evidence to support the accuser's position.

Sederer and Libby, as well as Gutheil, outlined several categories of false allegations that can occur:[8,9]

1. Exploitation: This category would include a patient who is blackmailing the doctor or a patient who was denied disability status and is seeking criminal redress or civil action against the doctor.
2. Retaliation: A retaliation claim could occur after the relationship between the patient and the doctor ends. The allegations in these types of claims may be of questionable merit because they are generally brought by the scorned lover to inflict pain.
3. Inadvertent stimulation of latent psychopathology: These claims come about when the patient's mental disorders cause a profound distortion of reality. An example of such a patient might include an adolescent female who was receiving therapy following a true case of incest. As opposed to confronting the true sexual abuser, the patient falsely accuses the doctor.

4. Competition with others: The patient may bring a false allegation against a therapist as a means of feeling that her or his relationship to the doctor is closer than that of other patients. The other patients may be real or fantasized.

5. Fantasy, or wish versus psychosis: Allegations of this type are made when the patient has such an intense desire for a sexual relationship with the therapist that it develops into a fantasy.

6. Money: A patient might bring allegations against a doctor simply as a way to make money. Schneidman observed, "As magically as a kiss can transform certain frogs into princes, a hug can change a patient into a plaintiff, a forty dollar motel room can become a one million dollar lawsuit overnight, and a hard-won career can vanish in smoke, never to reappear."[10]

Discriminating between true and false allegations of sexual misconduct is difficult even for a regulatory board experienced in assessing such claims. In a Missouri case, a regulatory board used polygraphic evidence to weigh the credibility of sexual misconduct allegations.[11] The use of such quasi-legal evidence by a board shows the extreme measures sometimes used in the emotionally charged cases of sexual misconduct.

■ Susceptibility of Chiropractic to Allegations of Sexual Misconduct

Chiropractic is distinct from other health-care professions in its philosophy and physical approach to care using the chiropractic adjustment. This physical approach to treatment may create opportunities for misunderstandings and violations of professional boundaries. As mentioned earlier, the incidence rate of disciplinary actions for sexual boundary violations is higher for chiropractors than for medical doctors. The underlying causes of the higher rate have yet to be adequately studied. Some possible explanations deserve mention and may be partially a result of the uniqueness of the profession.

Direct Skin Contact

Unlike some health-care professionals, chiropractors routinely gown their patients. Depending on the patient's condition, the chiropractor may treat numerous areas of the body during one session. For example, a patient with low-back pain with associated sciatica might receive both osseous and soft-tissue treatments of the calf, buttock, pelvis, and lumbar spine. The physical contact between chiropractor and patient during such treatments can be protracted, which could lead to misunderstandings and prompt complaints against the chiropractor.

Repetitive Nature of Chiropractic Treatment

The standard of chiropractic care, especially during the acute phase of treatment, is to treat the patient on multiple occasions. This frequency of care, usually several treatments per week, increases the opportunity for a misunderstanding to occur. In addition, repetitive office visits provide the opportunity for slow movement down the "slippery slope" of transference or countertransference.

Protracted Treatment Times

The reality of allopathic care in the twenty-first century is that a physician's time with a patient is usually quite limited. These brief encounters may protect both the medical doctor and patient by reducing the likelihood that sexual boundary violations will occur. Chiropractic care, in contrast, frequently requires long office visits.

The combination of long treatment times, frequent office visits, and close physical contact between doctor and patient may create increased opportunities for both simple misunderstandings, as well as actual sexual boundary violations.

Public Perceptions of Chiropractic Examinations

The public and other health-care professionals appear to have minimal understanding about the breadth and depth of a chiropractic education. Many erroneously conclude that chiropractors only examine the spine. In reality, programs approved by the Council on Chiropractic Education follow established competency criteria and require chiropractors to learn many examination procedures for regions besides the spine. For example, doctors of chiropractic are trained to examine the heart, lungs, and abdomen. Some states, such as California, require chiropractors to perform a minimum number of proctological and gynecological examinations to receive a license to practice.[12]

There is fertile ground for misunderstanding if a patient enters a chiropractic office with the idea that the doctor will only be examining the spine but the clinical investigation reveals the need to auscultate the abdomen for presence of an abdominal aneurysm.

Chiropractic Techniques

It is reasonable to assume that the public would associate chiropractic care with spinal manipulation. Manipulative procedures typically do not provoke misunderstandings of sexual misconduct because most patients assume that a chiropractor will be placing his or her hands on the neck and back. However, other chiropractic procedures could lead to misunderstandings between doctor and patient. An example of such a procedure is an internal coccyx adjustment. Many practicing chiropractors would agree that an internal coccyx adjustment is a legitimate, clinically helpful procedure in the properly diagnosed patient. Further, an internal coccyx adjustment is allowed in 85 percent of the United States.[13] Despite such widespread use, the procedure still has great potential for misunderstanding, and the suggestion of impropriety may always exist.

Other chiropractic procedures, which are used less often and allowed by fewer states, may carry an even higher degree of potential misunderstanding. A prime example is the practice of intravaginal uterine manipulation. While the procedure is allowed in 45 percent of the United States, it is unlikely that it is used by 45 percent of chiropractors.[14] It should be obvious that a chiropractor performing such a procedure is more likely to be misunderstood by patients. The well-intentioned doctor of chiropractic should consider conducting pretreatment discussions and using chaperones and other protective measures before performing an intravaginal uterine manipulation.

Endnotes

1. Summer GL, McCrory E. Professional sexual misconduct: the current reality, current concepts, ignorance is no excuse. Ala Med 1994;65:4–6.
2. Pope KS, Bouhoutsos JC. Sexual Intimacy Between Therapists and Patients. New York: Praeger, 1988.

3. Sexual misconduct statement of the Virginia board of medicine. W V Med J 1993;89:276–277.

4. Smith BD, Gutheil T. A patient's false claim of therapist sexual misconduct. Hosp Community Psychiatry 1993;44:793–794.

5. Sederer LI, Libby M. False allegations of sexual misconduct: clinical and institutional considerations. Psychiatr Serv 1995;46:160–163.

6. Hansen-Flaschen J, Adler BS. Allegations of sexual abuse in an intensive care unit. Crit Care Med 1999;27:437–440.

7. Stahl MJ, Foreman SM. Sexual Misconduct: Ethical, Clinical and Legal Ramifications and the Chiropractic Professions. Des Moines, IA: NCMIC, 1997.

8. Gutheil TG. Approaches to forensic assessment of false claims of sexual misconduct by therapists. Bull Am Acad Psychiatry Law 1992;20:289–296.

9. Sederer LI, Libby M. False allegations of sexual misconduct: clinical and institutional considerations. Psychiatr Serv 1995;46:160–163.

10. Schneidman BS. Sexual misconduct: the magic kiss. Federation Bulletin: The Journal of Medical Licensure and Discipline 1993;80:78–80.

11. Welty v State Board of Chiropractic Examiners, 759 SWW2d 295 (Mo Ct App 1988).

12. California Code of Regulations, Title 16, Division 4, State Board of Chiropractic Examiners, §331.12.2(e)(1).

13. Lam LD, Wegner E, Collord D. Chiropractic scope of practice: what the law allows. J Manip Phys Ther 1993;18:16–20.

14. Ibid.

Classifying Sexual Misconduct: A Chiropractic Paradigm

13

The objective of every visit to a health-care practitioner, regardless of the specialty, is to improve the patient's state of health. (A notable exception is hospice care, in which the clinical outcome is known and care is geared to make the patient as comfortable as possible.) How practitioners go about achieving this objective is largely predicated on their licensing and training. There are three basic processes to get a patient to a better state of health:

1. Enhance the body's own ability to heal: for example, physical therapy, chiropractic manipulative therapy, psychotherapy, acupuncture
2. Administer chemicals: for example, hormone replacement therapy, chemotherapy, antibiotics, steroids
3. Alter the anatomy: surgery

Some patients present with clinical conditions that allow for only one of the healing processes. For instance, a patient who sustains a pelvic fracture with associated internal bleeding would require immediate surgery rather than natural healing methods or drugs. On the other hand, some conditions allow for all three processes during a course of care.

A medical provider with a plenary license has the ability to use all three of the healing processes. The "talking" therapies of psychotherapy focus on improving health rather than alleviating sickness, which is the focus of the medical profession.[1] A chiropractor, who holds a non-plenary license, provides care that is also designed to restore patients' health by enhancing the body to increase its own healing processes. Chiropractic manipulative therapy, or the adjustment, represents the profession's primary form of health delivery and distinguishes chiropractic from all other health-care providers.

The unique health care delivered by the chiropractic profession calls for an equally unique paradigm by which to judge that care. Should the standards of dentistry be used to judge chiropractic?[2] The mental health provider requires transference to achieve a positive outcome. By contrast, the effectiveness of chiropractic manipulative therapy is not predicated on the degree of transference that may accompany the chiropractor-patient relationship. Because the chiropractic profession is unique among health-care professions, we condemn the use of other health-care paradigms in judging chiropractic care. The condemnation does not end there. The chiropractic profession should also be faulted for not fully embracing every opportunity to academically provide the public, legislators, and legal communities with reasonable and publicly acceptable standards of care that form the basis for professional trust. If this unique chiropractic profession does not give those who sit in judgment of its actions uniquely chiropractic standards, the models of other health-care providers *will* be used. This is very relevant in terms of the serious legal issues surrounding sexual misconduct.

The following sections presents a unique paradigm that specifically addresses the issue of sexual misconduct in the context of chiropractic care. Our recommendations are not meant to be a commentary as to the standards of either the medical or behavioral sciences. The authors acknowledge the uniqueness of those professions and standards that they have chosen to implement.

■ Fiduciary Relationships

Like all other health-care professions, chiropractic establishes a doctor-patient relationship that represents a prototypical fiduciary relationship. However, the power derived from the chiropractor-patient relationship is different from that of other providers and needs to be defined by a set of standards that apply only to the chiropractic profession.

■ Definition of Professional Boundaries

A banker-depositor is another type fiduciary relationship. Misconduct by a banker reflects improper implementation of financial responsibilities. The boundaries of chiropractic behavior are defined by clinical and nonclinical care, and misconduct occurs when the chiropractor did not act with the sole intent of getting the patient to a better state of health. In other words, a professional boundary is the proper clinical distance and respect that is afforded to a patient who has an established chiropractor-patient relationship.

■ Classifications of Sexual Misconduct

The chiropractic paradigm we propose places sexual misconduct into two divisions: nonphysical and physical contact between the chiropractor and patient.

Nonphysical Contact

Verbal and Written Communications and Gestures

This category includes speech, written material, and gestures made by a chiropractor that could offend the reasonable person. Examples include erotic statements, off-color jokes, sexually suggestive pictures, or gestures suggestive of erotic behavior. Such behavior should be considered unethical.

Electronic Media

This type of unprofessional conduct occurs when a chiropractor exploits a patient by wire or electronic means for self-gratification or commercial gain. It too should always be considered unethical.

Physical Contact with Patient: Nonsexual

This type of conduct represents the intentional act of touching the patient in a nonclinical manner for self-gratification and exploitation of the patient. The propriety of physical contact is based on whether the contact was purely clinical.

Sexual Contact

Sexual contact includes engaging in any conduct that is sexual, or may be reasonably interpreted as being sexual, including coital, oral/genital, oral/anal, or anal sex; masturbation; and sex using foreign objects. There are three subcategories: sexual relations under the guise of therapy, sexual relations with current patients, and sexual relations with former patients. There are no forms of chiropractic care that would include sexual relations with a patient as therapy. Such conduct should always be considered unethical. Almost all sexual contact concurrent with a chiropractor-patient relationship should be considered unethical. A possible mitigating factor is the legal standing of the relationship between the chiropractor and patient—for example, marriage or other relationships considered legally equivalent to marriage. Some states, such as California, provide this specific exception in their regulations.[3] Otherwise, a sexual relationship with a current patient should be considered unethical. Due to the controversy surrounding the ethical propriety of having a sexual relationship with a former patient, we propose a system that weighs several unique elements of the dilemma. Although other professions have adopted some generalized guidelines on this issue, currently no process of weighing evidence appears to be in place.[4]

■ A Weighted Method of Evaluating Sexual Relationships with Former Patients

We propose a weighted approach that is efficient, logical, and free of the inherent frailties of adopting zero-tolerance standards to all post-termination sexual relationships. With our weighted approach, all the elements that make up professional boundary issues are analyzed individually. Mitigating factors and intent can be considered independently for each issue. Then, looking at the totality of the evidence, a final determination can be made as to the merits of an allegation of sexual misconduct between a former patient and a chiropractor. Gutheil and

Gabbard commented, "The matter of context is all too often disregarded by fact finders and decision makers in this area, although it is essential to determine, *inter alia,* whether a specific behavior represents a boundary crossing or a boundary violation."[5]

Determining the level of power derived from the former chiropractor-patient relationship lies at the heart of our weighing process. The genesis of any inequality of power centers on the issues of transference and countertransference. The actions that argue for and against transference and countertransference determine the amount of weight that should be given to each factor described in the following sections.

Duration and Type of Care Provided

The duration and type of care provided to the patient have a direct bearing on the potential power derived from the former chiropractor-patient relationship. Transference does not generally occur when the course of care is short. Therefore, the duration of the former chiropractor-patient relationship should be identified and properly considered when evaluating the propriety of a sexual relationship with a former patient. If a chiropractor-patient relationship lasted only a few visits, it would be irrational to conclude that the patient developed a high degree of transference. As the potential for transference decreases, the likelihood of an equitable decision between two consenting adults to enter into a nonclinical relationship increases.

The type of physical condition necessitating the former chiropractor-patient relationship also requires evaluation. If the condition required straightforward medical decision making, transference would be less likely. Conversely, if the condition required the care and treatment of residual injuries from a spinal fracture, the potential for transference issues would be greater. When the potential for transference, or countertransference, is high, the chiropractor's decision to enter a nonclinical relationship with a former patient becomes suspect.

Circumstances Surrounding Termination of Care

The issue of how the former chiropractor-patient relationship ended centers on two questions: Did the chiropractor-patient relationship end as part of routine clinical treatment, or did care end with the intent of having a romantic or sexual relationship with the patient? If the relationship ended strictly on a clinical basis, the potential for transference and countertransference is minimal. However, if the care ended with the intent of initiating a nonclinical (sexual) relationship, further questions need to be answered. Did the care end abruptly to advance the nonclinical relationship? Was the patient being seen for a condition several times a week and then released without adequate transfer of care? Did the doctor initially recommend 30 visits only to end care after 10 visits, with no transfer of care? Answering these and other related questions will give insight into the possibility of a fraudulent termination as well the presence of transference and countertransference issues.

Statements or Actions of Chiropractor During the Course of Treatment

In trying to determine the power inequity derived from a former chiropractor-patient relationship, the statements made by the doctor during the course of care can be of value. Any erotic or suggestive statements made during the chiropractic-patient relationship might indicate the degree of countertransference present. Was the chiropractor, over the course of several visits, using the power of his/or her position as a fiduciary to contaminate the normal decision-making abilities of the patient?

Amount of Personal Information Chiropractor Gathered from Patient

Did the chiropractor gather a significant amount of personal information from the patient during the course of treatment? A sympathetic ear, coupled with clinical standing, equates to more power in the chiropractor-patient relationship. Revelations of personal information (e.g., a pending divorce, sexual fantasies, marital dissatisfaction) can accelerate transference.

Amount of Personal Information Chiropractor Disclosed to Patient

Inappropriate self-disclosure of personal information by the chiropractor would represent a loss of clinical objectivity. Telling a patient about an impending divorce or dissatisfaction with a spouse indicates that the doctor was using undue influence and that countertransference issues may have been present during the former chiropractor-patient relationship.

Former Patient's Personal History

Certain factors in a patient's medical history could give the arbitrator of an allegation of sexual misconduct insight on the potential for transference within the former chiropractor-patient relationship. Addictive behaviors (e.g., alcoholism, drug abuse, pathologic gambling), prior sexual abuse, or incest could make a patient more vulnerable.[6,7] Such vulnerability gives rise to transference.

Former Patient's Mental Status or Emotional Dependence

Any type of pathology associated with mental status has an effect on the patient being able to make prudent decisions. Borderline personalities and bipolar disorders are examples of mental conditions that would limit a patient's ability to make an uncontaminated decision to be romantically involved with a former chiropractor.[8,9]

Likelihood of Adverse Effects on Former Patient and Others

When evaluating the integrity of a nonclinical relationship between a chiropractor and a former patient, the harm, if any, that resulted from the relationship should also be determined and appropriately weighed. Has the patient made allegations of a boundary violation? Has the patient suffered emotional harm as a result of the relationship? Some people contend that all sexual relationships end with emotional trauma. Charlton concluded that the harm inflicted on a patient by sexual contact with a therapist is subjective and "it is difficult to assess to what extent the clients who have suffered sexual contact differ from the clients who have not."[10]

Amount of Time Passed Since Care Terminated

How much time has passed between termination of the chiropractic-patient relationship and initiation of the nonclinical relationship is one of the most widely used measures to determine the presence of transference. Although a so-called cooling-off period has been suggested by many authors and organizations, there is no consensus on exactly how long that period should be. However, the longer the chiropractor had no contact with the former patient, the more likely that any transference that may have been present would have dissipated.

Posttermination Contact

How did the chiropractic-patient meet following the termination of care? Was the posttermination meeting unrelated to the previous professional relationship? A serendipitous meeting, after care had been terminated, would indicate a more balanced and equitable personal relationship. Conversely, a doctor coming to the patient's home to initiate a personal relationship could indicate a high level of countertransference.

Rural Versus Urban Settings

Whether the chiropractor practices in a rural or urban setting should also be a determining factor when evaluating a chiropractor's sexual involvement with a former patient. Should the rural chiropractor who chooses to practice in a medically underserved community be penalized?

Australia, a sparsely populated country, has identified the gray areas surrounding the uniqueness of health care in a rural setting and has rejected zero-tolerance standards.[11] Zinn says, "You are suggesting that a young, unmarried doctor in a country town can never have any relationship with anyone in that town because every male and female in the town is a patient.... We must be aware of the shades of grey. The problem is not clear cut."

■ Mandatory Reporting

The chiropractic profession should have a unified voice demonstrating strong contempt for sexual misconduct and decrying those who are found guilty, either by criminal or regulatory boards, of committing sexual offenses. Further, all state professional societies should consider publishing disciplinary actions in their journals. Such publication could include the details of properly adjudicated evidence and all penalties, terms, and conditions of judgments.

Reporting allows colleagues who may be on the fringes of such unprofessional conduct to see the serious consequences of violating professional boundaries. For patients who have been abused by practitioners, these public disclosures might serve as encouragement to come forward and provide a level of personal vindication.

■ Conclusions

The intent of this book is to present a comprehensive multidisciplinary international review on the subject of sexual misconduct. By identifying many of the social and cultural influences that have led to the current zero-tolerance standards adopted by other health-care professions, we hope to have shown parallels to the chiropractic profession.

It would be erroneous to conclude that this book is an attempt to give safe harbor to those who commit sexual misconduct and claim it to be a form of legitimate chiropractic care. Some readers might also conclude that throwing stones at glass houses of, admittedly well-intended, zero-tolerance standards is an attempt to give wider latitude to those who have moral and ethical deficits. This too would be another erroneous conclusion.

Academic integrity and bravery comes to those who will point out the frailties of common belief. This book is an attempt to point out the weaknesses of thought and standards that are being thrown on the chiropractic profession. The recommendations we make for the chiropractic profession represent truly enforceable standards of conduct that will better serve the public as well as the profession.

The only way to seize control of the current social, political, and legal agendas adopting zero-tolerance standards—like those used in suspending a kindergarten student for bringing a plastic ax to school—is to adopt a strict intolerance of actions that clearly represent professional misconduct. A determination of sexual misconduct must be made using a thorough knowledge and understanding of the unique standard of care provided by the chiropractic profession.

The backbone of any determination of sexual misconduct is the integrity of the chiropractic profession. Leaders at the regulatory level as well as within professional and educational entities must require professional conduct that is above reproach. More importantly, the individual practitioners must recognize the importance of personal integrity.

In 1986, Dr. W. Webb, then chairman of the American Psychiatry Association Ethics Committee, made the following comments regarding his profession's need for professional integrity.[12] The chiropractic profession would also do well to acknowledge the power inherent in professional personal integrity.

> In the final analysis, the integrity of our profession lies in the integrity of our individual practitioners. We must continually remind ourselves of the power of the doctor-patient relationship. The power that offers the capacity to heal contains the capacity to cloud therapeutic objectivity. In the covenant with our patients we realize our greatest therapeutic potential. Threats to the covenant damage our basic professional integrity.

Endnotes

1. Charlton BG. Sexual ethics in psychiatry. Curr Opin Psychiatry 1993;6:713–716.
2. Jorgenson L, Hirsch A. Sexual contact between dentist and patient: is dating ethical? CDS Rev 1994;87:24–27.
3. California Code of Regulations, Title 16, Division 4, State Board of Chiropractic Examiners, §316(c).
4. Keith Spiegel P, Koocher G. Ethics in Psychology. New York: Random House, 1985.
5. Gutheil TG, Gabbard GO. Misuses and misunderstandings of boundary theory in clinical and regulatory settings. Am J Psychiatry 1998;155:409–414.
6. Carnes P, Schneider JP. Recognition and management of addictive sexual disorders: guide for the primary care clinician. Lippincotts Prim Care Pract 2000;4:302–318.
7. Webb WL. The doctor-patient covenant and the threat of exploitation. Am J Psychiatry 1986;143:1149–1150.
8. Gutheil TG. Borderline personality disorder, boundary violations and patient-therapist sex: medicolegal pitfalls. Am J Psychiatry 1989;146:597–602.
9. Collins D. Sexual involvement between psychiatric hospital staff and their patients. In: Gabbard G, ed. Sexual Exploitation in Professional Relationships. Washington, DC: American Psychiatric Press, 1989.
10. Charlton BG. 6:713–716.
11. Zinn C. Australian doctors get tough on sexual misconduct. BMJ 1994;308:1185–1186.
12. Webb WL. The doctor-patient covenant and the threat of exploitation. Am J Psychiatry 1986;143:1149–1150.

Responses to Power Poll Conducted by the Federation of Chiropractic Licensing Boards

APPENDIX

A

FEDERATION OF CHIROPRACTIC LICENSING BOARDS
Summary of Power Poll Responses

The FCLB needs your help to assist in a research project by Dr. Steve Foreman that may help all member boards.   9/9/2002 0:00

Question #1 Does your board have statutes or regulations concerning doctor/patient sexual relations?
Yes   No

Question #2 Do your regulations specifically prohibit sexual relations between the doctor and patients who are active or currently under care?
Yes   No

Question #3 Do your regulations specifically prohibit sexual relations between the doctor and patients who are inactive or formerly under care?
Yes   No   If yes, how long is the doctor prohibited from having sexual relations with former patients?

Question #4 Do your regulations specify any measures that must take place before a chiropractor can have romantic or sexual involvement with a former patient? Examples would include time periods, referrals to other doctors, counseling, etc.
Yes - measures include _____ No

Question #5 Do your regulations delineate any categories of other prohibited conduct such as improper comments of a sexual nature?

Yes - prohibited conduct _____ No

Question #6   Do your regulations address any other methods of contact between the doctor and patient, in terms of sexually inappropriate behavior? Examples would include video, audio, and telephone conversations for "phone sex" or e-mail or chat rooms on the Internet.

Yes - prohibited contact _____ No

16-JAN-03	QUESTION #1	QUESTION #2	QUESTION #3	QUESTION #4	QUESTION #5	QUESTION #6
AL	No	No	No	No	No	No
AK	Yes	Yes	No	No	Yes, "lewd or immoral conduct"	See attached regs.
AZ	Yes	Yes	Yes, sexual relationship cannot have started after the doctor/patient relationship was established.	No	Yes, suggesting sexual contact	No
AR	Yes	Yes	No	Yes, see website Rules & Regs pg 6 (p)		
CA	Yes	Yes	No	No	No. www.chiro.ca.gov Regs Sec 316 c	
CO	Yes. Statutes.	Yes	Yes, 6 mos immed following termination	Yes, see statute attached.	Yes, as defined in CRS 18-3-401	As defined in CRS 18-3-401
CT	Statutes do not specifically reference sexual misconduct, but sexual misconduct is considered to be "illegal, negligent or incompetent" practice and therefore a violation of the standard of care. In such cases, the standard of care is established through testimony and other evidence (e.g. ethics codes). The Board may also rely on the precedent of past cases which establish the standard of care. Such conduct may also be criminal activity under certain circumstances.					
DE	Yes	No	No	No	6.3 R&R- "unprofessional conduct"	Yes, "unprofessional conduct"

(*continued*)

LAST REVISED: (Continued)						
16-JAN-03	QUESTION #1	QUESTION #2	QUESTION #3	QUESTION #4	QUESTION #5	QUESTION #6
DC	No		No	No	Yes, regs (statute) prohibits sexual harassment of a patient or client.	No, except as such would be considered sexual harassment
FL	Yes		No	Yes, after 1 yr of non-treatment	Yes, suggestive remarks or conduct	No
GA	Yes	Yes	Yes, 6 months	Yes	No	No. Not addressed.
HI	Yes	Yes	No, refers to patient only without qualifying inactive or formerly.	No	Yes, intercourse, masturbation, prostitution, making suggestive, lewd, lascivious, or improper advances to a patient	No
ID						
IL						
IN	Yes	No	No	No	No	No
IA	No, law prohibits engaging in unethical conduct or practice harmful or detrimental to the public.	No, rules specify as grounds for discipline any actions that are classified as incompetent, unethical, or inappropriate conduct under which of these noted ones would fall comment in #6.	No	No	No	#1 & 2 apply to all questions. Note that all of the types of sexual misconduct would be a violation of Bd's ethic prof practice/disc rules & would be construed as grounds for discipline under Bd's statute and disc rules.
KS						

(*continued*)

KY	Yes, see attached 312.150.	"Moral turpitude" attached.				No
LA	No	Yes	No	No	No	No
ME	Yes		No	No	Yes, kissing, inappropriate touching, masturbation, "sexual favors"	Yes, any conversation of a sexual nature that is not related to a patient's complaints, "sexual fantasies," discussion of sexual preferences, soliciting a date or romance. See Chapter 7, Sec 4, Item D of rules on Web page.
MD	Yes	Yes	No	No	No	
MA	Yes	Yes	Yes, 90 days.	Yes. (233 CMR 4.06(n)) 90 days after "...professional consultation, diagnostic service or therapeutic service..."	Yes. (233 CMR 4.06(o)) "Inducing... any patient to submit to any form of sexual relationship, activity or contact by falsely representing that the sexual relationship, activity or contact will, or may be of diagnostic or therapeutic benefit."	No. 233 CMR 4.01 "Internal [gyn]" exam prohibited.

LAST REVISED: (Continued)

16-JAN-03	QUESTION #1	QUESTION #2	QUESTION #3	QUESTION #4	QUESTION #5	QUESTION #6
MI						
MN	Yes	Yes	No, currently developing language, 2 yrs after last treatment/visit.	No	Yes, "prohibited ...engaging in conduct with a patient that is sexual or may reasonably be interpreted by the patient as sexual, or in any verbal behavior that is seductive or sexually demeaning to a patient"	No. See statute 148.10, subd 1(a)(11)(b) at www.mn-chiro board.state.mn.us.
MS	Yes	Yes	Yes, 2 yrs	Yes, 2 yrs	No	No
MO	Yes	No	No	No	No	No. See attached statutory language.
MT	Yes	Yes	No	No	Yes, sexual misconduct either verbal or physical, sexual contact, sexual exploitation or	See #5 (exploitation).

(continued)

State						
NE	Yes	Yes	No	No	Yes	sex offense as defined in 45-2-101, MCA, when such act or solicitation is related to the practice of chiropractic
NV	Yes	Yes	Yes, a reasonable time	Yes, after doctor/patient relationship has been terminated for a reasonable time	No	Yes, verbal or physical conduct of a sexual nature requesting sexual favors.
NH					No	Yes, "...conduct sexual in nature or may reasonably be interpreted as being sexual in nature, including without limitation, behavior, gestures and expressions that may reasonably be interpreted as being sexually suggestive or sexually demeaning to the patient"

LAST REVISED: *(Continued)*

16-JAN-03	QUESTION #1	QUESTION #2	QUESTION #3	QUESTION #4	QUESTION #5	QUESTION #6
NJ	Yes. See regs attached.	Yes	Yes, Dr/patient relationship must be actively terminated by notation in patient records and written notice to the patient or may be pursued if last professional service was rendered more than three months prior.	Yes. See #3.	Yes, no discussion of an intimate sexual nature unless related to legitimate patient needs. Includes discussion by licensee of his/her own intimate sexual relationships. Sexual harassment is defined in the regs and prohibited. Activity which would lead the reasonable person to believe that the activity serves the licensee's personal prurient interest, is for sexual arousal or the sexual gratification of the licensee or patient.	No, have instituted disciplinary action against a licensee who instant-messaged a patient and sent nude pictures of himself to the patient over the Internet.

NM

NY	Yes	No	No	No	Yes, "Willfully harassing, abusing or intimidating a patient either physically or verbally..."	No. Bd is drafting guidelines for preventing sexual misconduct.
NC	No. Only refers to lewd and immoral conduct toward a patient.		No	No	No	No
ND	Yes	No	No	No	No	No
OH	See attached 4734-9-06	No	No	No	No	No
OK	Yes	Yes	No	No	No	No
OR	Yes	Yes	Yes, see OAR 811-035-0015(1)(D).	Yes, OAR811-035-0015(1)(D)	Yes, OAR811-035-0015(1)(a)-(e)	Yes, "any conduct or verbal behavior..." Attached.
PA						
RI						
SC	Yes	Yes	Yes, 3 mos. following care	No	No	No
SD	Yes	Yes	No	No	No	No
TN	Yes					
TX	Yes	Yes	Yes, 6 mos. from last visit	Yes, "No longer emotionally dependent" and 6 mos. terminated professional relationship	Yes, sexual impropriety (gestures, comments, request to date, etc.) and sexual intimacy (broad definition)	No

(continued)

16-JAN-03	QUESTION #1	QUESTION #2	QUESTION #3	QUESTION #4	QUESTION #5	QUESTION #6
UT	Yes, regs	Yes	Yes, 12 mos. from last treatment	No	Yes, with or without consent if risk of exploitation or potential harm	No
VT	Yes	Yes	No	No	Yes, "sexual harassment of patient"	No
VA	See attached Regulations					
WA	Yes, WAC 246-808-590. 1-Chiropractor shall never engage in sexual contact or sexual activity with current clients. 2-Chiro shall never engage in sexual contact or sexual activity with former clients if such contact or activity involves the abuse of the Chiro/client relationship. Factors which the commission may consider in evaluating if the chiro/client relationship has been abusive include but are not limited to: a) amount of time passed since therapy terminated; b) nature and duration of the therapy; c) circumstances of cessation or termination; d) former client's personal history; e) former client's current mental status; f) likelihood of adverse impact on the former client and others; g) any statements or actions made by the chiro during the course of treatment suggesting or inviting the possibility of a post-termination sexual or romantic relationship with former client. 3-Chiro shall never engage in sexually harassing or demeaning behavior with current or former clients.					
WV	Yes	Yes	Yes, 6 months after termination of doctor/patient relationship.	Sexual misconduct may include, doctor/patient relations, whether or not initiated by, or consented to, by thepatient, and engaging in any conduct with a patient that is sexual or may be reasonably interpreted as sexual. A licensee shall not use fraud, deception, misrepresentation or force for the purpose of engaging in sexual contact with a patient in the clinical setting. Patient consent is not a legal defense.		

WI	Yes	Yes	No	Yes	Yes. "Engaging in sexual contact, exposure, gratification, or other sexual behavior with or in the presence of a patient . . ."	No
WY	Yes	Yes	No	No	Yes	No
Puerto Rico						
US Virgin Is.						
Alberta						
British Col.	Yes	Yes	Yes, once the patient understands the chiro/patient relationship has ended	Yes, must not be a patient.	Yes	Yes
Manitoba						
New Brunswick						
Newfoundland/ Labrador						
Nova Scotia						
Ontario						
Pr. Edward Is.						
Quebec						
Saskatchewan						
New So. Wales						
Victoria						

Role of State Chiropractic Regulatory Boards in Protecting the Public

APPENDIX

B

Members of state regulatory boards are charged with the responsibility of protecting the public, in part by making decisions regarding chiropractors who have committed boundary violations. They are afforded great power and latitude in making decisions because of the power doctors have over patients through the fiduciary relationship. Many board members find themselves asking, "Would I send my spouse, parent or child to this doctor? If not, how can I allow others to seek care in his/her office?"

The boards' decision-making processes are complicated, but the responsibility would be lessened somewhat by the comfort of consistency in their decisions. To that end, we offer some recommendations that may help bring consistency to board decisions in the areas of punishment, protection, rehabilitation, and testing.

■ Punishment Decisions

The decisions of state and national chiropractic boards are designed to punish doctors for misconduct. Applicable options include citations or public reprimands, monetary fines, license suspension, stayed revocation of a license with probationary terms and conditions, and complete revocation.

Sometimes a board can reach a decision easily on hearing the facts of the case. In some instances, regulations mandate revocation. In other cases—for instance, those involving sexual acts with children, predatory behavior, and violent acts such as rape—the doctor's behavior is sufficiently egregious that revocation is the only true option that ensures public protection.

Decisions with lesser punishments are usually more difficult to make because they involve a less serious boundary violation and the facts are less clear. These cases are suitable for probation and license restrictions.

■ Protection Decisions

Some board decisions are based more on protecting the unsuspecting public than on punishing the doctor. Of course, the ultimate protection decision is license revocation, which eliminates the doctor's ability to treat any patient. However, most protection decisions are centered on specific restrictions as a condition of a probationary license. Examples include not allowing the treatment of minors or children under a specific age. Other commonly encountered restrictions include not allowing the doctor to treat patients of the opposite sex for a specific period. Once the specified period has passed, the doctor must undergo psychological evaluation before regaining the ability to treat patients of the opposite sex.

■ Rehabilitation Decisions

In many cases, the facts support some level of punishment, such as probation for a specific number of months or years, as well as some protection decisions, such as a restricted license during probation. Often board members also desire to make decisions that will assist the doctor and provide some degree of rehabilitation through education. Despite the desirability of rehabilitation in many cases, boards use this option infrequently because of difficulties in the following areas:

- *Course location.* Often there is no chiropractic college in the state that can offer a course in close proximity. Extreme distance makes repeated visits to the closest chiropractic college campus impractical.
- *Course availability.* Rehabilitation courses are not readily available at chiropractic colleges. If they are offered, they are usually

available only certain times in the year, and the doctor may have to wait many months before the next offering.

- *Course content.* Many courses on ethics or sexual boundaries are not designed with the chiropractor in mind. In fact, most such courses are designed for the workplace and have nothing to do with health care.
- *Course depth.* Most courses are designed to give additional information to doctors who have not been accused or found guilty of sexual improprieties. Clearly, their message is more informational and preventative than rehabilitative. Doctors who have been disciplined for sexual boundary violations require a far more pointed discussion that has the ability to alter the doctor's behavior.

■ Testing Decisions

At the time of this writing, board members have very few testing options for doctors who have committed sexual boundary violations. The few courses available on boundary issues do not typically have testing modules. The National Board of Chiropractic Examiners (NBCE) has used the Special Purposes Examination in Chiropractic (SPEC) test for a number of years, but the test is designed to assess the current level of clinical competency of doctors who have been disciplined or unlicensed for a length of time. Although the SPEC does assess doctors who have ethical problems, the NBCE is currently developing a test specifically for ethics and boundary issues.

As noted, state boards have traditionally handed down decisions that combine punishment of the doctor and protection of the public in cases involving boundary violations and sexual misconduct. The challenge is that boards receive large numbers of complaints and do not take disciplinary action in every case. Many cases are either dropped due to limited proof or facts, and others result in warning letters. When a board does not take disciplinary action, an attempt to change the doctor's behavior through remedial education could have long-term benefit to the doctor and serve to protect the public. Specific remediation courses have recently been developed and are available for board use at CEvantive.com.

Glossary

Absolute morality. A set of principles or rules of conduct based on the belief that a behavior is either totally right or totally wrong. No situational influences are allowed to create gray areas.

Beyond a reasonable doubt. A standard of evidence used in criminal trials. This is the highest level of evidence required in court and would equate to approximately 90% of the evidence indicating guilt or innocence.

Bipolar disorder. Also known as manic-depressive illness; a brain disorder that causes unusual shifts in a person's mood, energy, and ability to function.

Boundary crossing. A brief excursion across professional boundaries followed by a rapid return to established limits of the professional relationship.

Boundary violation. A breach of professional boundaries in which the practitioner sets personal needs above those of the patient.

Clear and convincing evidence. The level of evidence required in an administrative trial. It lies between a preponderance of evidence and beyond a reasonable doubt and equates to approximately 75% of the evidence indicating guilt or innocence.

Countertransference. The transference of emotions and/or feelings to the patient by the therapist or doctor.

Dual relationship. A relationship between a doctor and a patient that has more than one basis; for example, a business relationship and a social relationship carried on along with the doctor-patient relationship.

Fiduciary. A person to whom property or power is entrusted for the benefit of another.

Hippocratic oath. An oath, thought to have been written by Hippocrates, that was adopted by early Christian physicians. It states, in part, "with purity and holiness I will practice my art. . . . Into whatever house I enter I will go into them for the benefit of the sick and will abstain from every voluntary act of Mischief and Corruption and further from the seduction of females or males, freemen and slaves."

Loss of consortium. The legal term used a suit that attempts to recover damages suffered by a person for the loss of intimate relations with a spouse.

Mesmerism. Hypnosis as induced by F. A. Mesmer through animal magnetism.

Nonplenary license. A license restricted in terms of legally allowed treatment and scope of practice. Examples include a dental, podarthritic, or chiropractic license.

Plenary license. A license that is full, unlimited, and unrestricted in terms of scope of practice. Examples include the license of a medical or osteopathic physician.

Preponderance of the evidence. The level of evidence required to obtain a legal victory in a civil trial. It would equate to a 49% to 51% weighing of the evidence.

Professional boundary. The proper clinical distance and respect afforded to a patient who has an established doctor-patient relationship.

Professional sexual misconduct. A breach of trust and a violation of the professional's fiduciary responsibility to the patient. Marked by behavior that is seductive, demeaning, or harassing, or any behavior than a patient might reasonably interpret as sexual.

Sexual impropriety. Nonphysical, inappropriate conduct by a doctor toward a patient, who would consider such conduct disrespectful and demeaning.

Sexual transgression. Inappropriate physical contact between doctor and patient, stopping short of an overt sexual act.

Sexual violation. A sexual act between doctor and patient, not limited to coitus but including oral sex, anal intercourse, and mutual masturbation.

Transference. An unconscious assignment of feelings and attitudes of important figures in the past to persons in the present.

Transition zone. The area in the clinical setting where the patient transitions from the treatment area to exiting area.

Zero tolerance. A school of thought that allows no level of toleration or acceptance of specified behaviors and considers no situational influences on an issue.

INDEX

Page numbers set in italics denote figures; those followed by a t denote tables.

Adkins, E., 52
Akamatsu, J. T., 19
Allegations, scope of, 31
American Chiropractic Association (ACA)
    Code of Ethics, 14–15
    dual relationships, 66
American College of Obstetricians and
    Gynecologists, 43, 57–58
American Medical Association (AMA)
    AMA Council Report, 4
    Council on Ethical and Judicial Affairs,
      57
    Current Procedural Terminology, 41
    sexual misconduct, 13–14
American Nursing Association (ANA), 14
American Psychiatry Association, 58, 102
American Psychological Association
    Revisions Task Force, 14, 62
    sexual misconduct, 14
Appelbaum, P. S., 62

Bailey, S., 22
Banales, J. Manuel, 4
Board of Licensed Professional Counselors
    and Therapists, 23–24
Borruso, M. T., 76
Boston, Archdiocese of, 30
Boston Globe, 30
Bouhoutsos, J. C., 18, 85
Boundary, professional
    defined, 52
    regulation, 63–64
    violations, 6, 7, 18, 50–51
Breuer, Joseph, 10–11
Brodsky, A. M., 18, 19, 45
Brown, L. S., 62
Brown, Lindsay, 2

Budnick. N., 23–24
Bush, George H., 28

California, 62
Campbell, D. C., 4, 34, 76
Canadian Medical Association (CMA)
    Code of Ethics, 14
    standards, 58
Canadian Psychiatric Association, 58, 60
Carr, M. L., 21
Catholic Church, 28, 30, 34
CBS, 3–4
Charlton, B. G., 99
Chiropractic
    allegations, susceptibility to, 88–90
    countertransference, 46–47
    criminal litigation, 74–75
    doctor-patient relationship, terminating,
      65–66
    examination, risk management during,
      80–83
    nonplenary licensing, 39, 41, 93
    relationships, fiduciary, 94
    and relationships of power, 42–43
    risk management, 79–80, 84–86
    sexual misconduct, 14–15, 22–24, 62–64,
      76
    sexual misconduct, false allegations of,
      87
    standards, need for, 94, 101–102
    transference, 46
    transition zone, 49
    treatment, risk management during,
      83–84
Ciramella, Janet, 3
Clinton, Bill, 28, 29–30, 31, 54
College of Nurses of Ontario, 21–22

College of Physicians and Surgeons of Alberta, Canada, 54–55
College of Physicians and Surgeons of Ontario, 60
Colorado, 62
Contraception, 4
Corpus Hippocratum, 9
Council on Chiropractic Education, 89
Counselors, mental health, 19
Curtisville Elementary (West Deer, Pa.), 3

Dehlendorf, C. E., 19–20
District of Columbia Circuit Court, Court of Appeals, 28
Dror, O., 22
Drugs, 3
Dry Creek Elementary School (Centennial, Colo.), 2

Ed Sullivan Show, The, 4
Equal Employment Opportunity Commission (EEOC), 28

Federation of Chiropractic Licensing Boards (FCLB), 15, 63
Feldstein, M., 18–19
Ferenczi, Sandor, 11
Florida, 58, 62
Foreman, S., 22
Forer, B. R., 18
Freud, Sigmund, 10, 11
Fualaau, Vili, 28–29
Fuller, M., 18

Gabbard, G. O., 53, 97
Galletly, C. A., 19
Gallop, R., 21–22
Gartrell, N., 18–19
Gartrell, N. K., 20–21, 53
Geoghan, John, 30
Goodson, W. H., 20–21
Greenberg, M., 18
Guidelines, cultural basis for, 27–28, 31, 60
Gutheil, T. G., 46, 53, 87, 96–97

Health care
    fiduciary relationships, 35–37, 49
    inpatient, 39, 41
    outpatient, 39, 41
    residential, 39, 41, 93
    rural, 59–60
    sexual misconduct, 3
    types of, 40t
    zero tolerance policy, application of, 6
Herman, J. L., 18–19, 60–61
Hess, Taylor, 2
Hill, Anita, 28, 31
Hippocratic Oath, 9–10, 51
Holroyd, J. C., 18
Hugging, 53
Human Sexual Inadequacy (Masters and Johnson), 11
Human Sexual Response (Masters and Johnson), 11
Hypnosis, 10–11

Intent, 2, 33, 34
International Chiropractic Association (ICA), 15

Jackson, Janet, 4
Johnson, Virginia, 74
    Human Sexual Inadequacy (Masters and Johnson), 11
    Human Sexual Response (Masters and Johnson), 11
    sex surrogacy, 60
Jones, Ernest, 10
Jones, L. E., 52
Jones, Paula, 30
Jorgenson, L., 62, 76

Kanka, Megan, 5
Kardener, S. H., 18, 60
Kissinger, Henry, 31
Kroll, J., 27
Kussin, D., 21

Law, Cardinal Bernard, 30
Legislation
    Gun-Free Schools Act of 1994, 2, 5
    Megan's Law, 5
    Violence Against Women Act of 1994, 74–75
Lerman, H., 18
Letourneau, Mary Kay, 28–29
Levenson, H., 18
Lewinsky, Monica, 28, 29–30, 31, 54
Libby, M., 87
Licensing
    nonplenary, 39, 41, 93
    plenary, 39, 93
    state regulatory boards, 73–74
Litigation
    civil, 71–73
    criminal, 74–77

increase in, 27
malpractice, 72–74
Roy v. Hartogs, 11–12
Utah Court of Appeals, 66
Lo, B., 20
Localio, R., 18–19
Locke, Jordan, 2–3
Louis XVI, king of France, 10

McCrory, E., 51–52, 84
Malpractice, 72–74
Marmor, Judd, 11
Masters, William, 74
  Human Sexual Inadequacy (Masters and
    Johnson), 11
  Human Sexual Response (Masters and
    Johnson), 11
  sex surrogacy, 60
Medical Council of New Zealand, 54, 55
Medication, 39, 41
Mensh, I. N., 18
Mesmer, Franz, 10
Milliken, N., 20–21
Morris, Seamus, 3
Morrison, J., 22–23

Neuro Emotional Technique (NET), 76
New Zealand, Medical Council of, 54, 55
Nurse practitioners, 41
Nursing, 14, 21–22

Obstetrics and gynecology
  and relationships of power, 43
  sexual misconduct, 18, 20, 21
Olarte, S., 18–19

Panetta, Leon, 29
Paraprofessionals (*see also* nursing)
  and relationships of power, 39
Parsons, J., 19, 22
Physicians, allopathic, 7, 17, 39, 89
  and relationships of power, 41
Physicians, behavioral, 7, 10–12, 14, 17
  incidence reports, 18–19, 21, 22
  and relationships of power, 41–42
  sexual misconduct, false allegations of, 87
Physicians, family practice, 20
Physicians, general practice, 18, 20
Physicians, internal medicine, 18, 20
Physicians, sexual misconduct by, 19–20,
    22–23, 76
Physicians assistants, 41
Pipes, R. B., 66–67
Pollack, W. S., 31

Pope, K. S., 18, 36–37, 46, 85
Presley, Elvis, 3–4
Psychiatry
  and relationships of power, 39
  sexual misconduct, 18–19, 20, 21, 72, 76
Psychology
  and relationships of power, 39
  sexual misconduct, 14, 18, 19, 22, 72
Psychotherapy, 10–12, 13, 45–46, 50, 62, 76,
    87, 93

Rape, 4, 29
Rapp, M. S., 60
Regulation, 59–60, 61–63
  California, 64, 90–91, 96
  Connecticut, 64
  Iowa, 64
  Nevada, 64
  state law, 76
  state regulatory boards, 73–74
  Texas, 64
Reich, Wilhelm, 11
Relationships
  dual, 36–37, 66
  fiduciary, 35–37, 42, 45, 49, 52, 94–95
  nonsexual, 66–67
  of power, 14, 28, 31, 36, 39, 41–43, 45, 51,
    97
Research, methodology of, 6–7, 17
Richards, J., 22
Robinson, G. E., 21, 50
Roy v. Hartogs, 11–12
Royal Australian and New Zealand College
    of Psychiatrists, 58
Rubin, S. S., 22

Schneidman, B. S., 88
Schover, L. R., 18
Searight, H. R., 4, 34, 76
Sederer, L. I., 87
Sex education, 4
Sex offenders
  notification, 5
  registration of, 4, 34
Sex surrogacy, 60–61
Sexual harassment, 52
Sexual misconduct
  Australia, 22, 60
  Canada, 21–22
  Catholic Church, 28, 30, 34
  chiropractic, 22–24
  classification of, 53–55, 94, 95–96
  counselors, mental health, 19
  criminalization of, 34, 74–77

defined, 4, 71
evalution of, 96–100
false allegations of, 86–88
incidence reports, 17–23, 100–101
Israel, 22
New Zealand, 60
nursing, 21–22
obstetrics and gynecology, 18, 20, 21
physicians, 19–20, 22–23
physicians, family practice, 20
physicians, general practice, 18, 20
physicians, internal medicine, 18, 20
psychiatry, 18–19, 20, 21, 72
psychology, 14, 19, 22, 72
psychotherapy, 10–12, 13
as rape, 4, 29, 74
and relationships of power, 43
reporting, 19
social workers, 19
by specialty, 20t, 23t
spectrum of, 51–52
surgeons, 18, 20
terminology, 52–54, 59
therapists, family, 19
therapists, marriage, 19
transition zone, 49–50
United States, 18–21, 22, 60
zero tolerance policy, application of,
    3, 5–6
Sheets, V. R., 53
Shopland, S. N., 61
Simon, R. I., 53, 59, 72
Simon, T. I., 50
Social workers
  and relationships of power, 39
  sexual misconduct, 19
Society of Obstetricians and Gynecologists
    (Canada), 58
Stahl, M., 22
Standards
  absolute morality, 33–34, 42, 45, 61
  current, 1–5, 57–59, 61
  historical, 9–10
  zero tolerance policy, application of, 2–3

Stewart, D. E., 21, 50
Summer, G. L., 51–52, 84
Super Bowl XXXVIII (2004), 4
Surgeons, sexual misconduct by,
    18, 20

Taylor Elementary School (Colorado
    Springs, Colo.), 3
Tennessee, 62
Therapists, family
  and relationships of power, 39
  sexual misconduct, 19
Therapists, marriage
  and relationships of power, 39
  sexual misconduct, 19
Thiemann, S., 20–21
Thomas, Clarence, 28

10th U.S. Circuit Court of Appeals,
    75
U.S. Constitution, 58, 59
U.S. Senate, Judiciary Committee,
    28
U.S. Supreme Court, 75

VandeCreek, L., 61
Violence, 2–3

Weapons, 2–3, 34
Webb, W., 102
West Virginia Board of Medicine,
    58, 85
Wickersham, P., 22–23
Wincze, J. P., 19, 22, 59–60
Wolfe, S., 19–20

Zero tolerance
  as policy, 30
  as policy, application of, 2–3,
    5–6, 53
Zero tolerance policy
  drugs, 3, 33
  violence, 2–3
  weapons, 2–3, 33, 34